# Jumbo Crosswords

100 puzzles

Book 2

Published by Richardson Publishing Group Limited
www.richardsonpublishinggroup.com

10 9 8 7 6 5 4 3 2 1



All puzzles supplied by Clarity Media

Cover design by Junior London

ISBN 978-1-913602-20-8

Printed and bound by Bell & Bain Ltd, 303 Burnfield Road, Thornliebank, Glasgow G46 7UQ



A catalogue record for this book is available from the British Library.

If you would like to comment on any aspect of this book, please contact us at:

E-mail: puzzles@richardsonpublishinggroup.com

Follow us on Twitter @puzzlesandgames
instagram.com/richardsonpuzzlesandgames
facebook.com/richardsonpuzzlesandgames

# Contents



# Instructions

Write the answers to each of the clues in the grid to complete the crossword puzzle.

# Crosswords

*No. 1*

## Across

- **1** Accidents (7)
- **5** Signal (anag.) (6)
- **8** Tunnel under a road for pedestrians (6)
- **11** Seed of an apple (3)
- **12** Suggestion (4)
- **13** Remorseful (9)
- **14** Goes in (6)
- **15** Elaborate (9)
- **16** Temporary inability to remember something (6,5)
- **20** Costume worn to a themed party (5,5)
- **21** The direct opposite of a thing (9)
- **24** Not ostentatious (13)
- **29** Jail (6)
- **31** Decorative design style (3,7)
- **33** Serendipitous (10)
- **35** Humorously sarcastic (6)
- **36** Boxing class division (13)
- **40** Large breed of dog (5,4)
- **42** Rival contestant (10)
- **44** Freed (11)
- **48** Protect from harm (9)
- **50** Fill a balloon with air (4,2)
- **51** Diffidence (9)
- **52** Wild mountain goat (4)
- **53** Young newt (3)
- **54** Relating to stars (6)
- **55** Curved (6)
- **56** More saccharine (7)

## Down

- **2** Alphabetical list (5)
- **3** Star performer (9)
- **4** Flight attendant (7)
- **5** Accord; consensus (9)
- **6** Narrow strip of land (7)
- **7** Flatten on impact (5)
- **8** Magical incantation (5)
- **9** Asian pepper plant (5)
- **10** Structure resembling an ear (7)
- **17** Approaches (5)
- **18** Performs in a play (4)
- **19** Involving two elements (9)
- **20** More delicate (5)
- **22** Dance club (5)
- **23** Transmits (5)
- **25** Vain (9)
- **26** Christmas (4)
- **27** Accustom (5)
- **28** Not in good physical condition (5)
- **30** Woody plant (4)
- **31** Chopping (5)
- **32** The ones over there (5)
- **34** Wedding official (5)
- **36** Collection of ships (5)
- **37** A house and outbuildings (9)
- **38** Tending to get in the way (9)
- **39** Distort (4)
- **41** Makes a continuous deep sound (7)
- **42** Offensively discourteous (7)
- **43** Personal belongings (7)
- **45** More recent (5)
- **46** Urge into action (5)
- **47** Main artery (5)
- **49** Pass a rope through (5)

*No. 1*

1 2 3 4 5 6 7 8 9 10 11 12 13 14 15 16 17 18 19 20 21 22 23 24 25 26 27 28 29 30 31 32 33 34 35 36 37 38 39 40 41 42 43 44 45 46 47 48 49 50 51 52 53 54 55 56

*No. 2*

## Across

**9** Contriving to bring about (11)
**10** Illustrations that aid understanding (8)
**12** Hesitant (9)
**13** Strikingly different (11)
**14** Plummet (8)
**16** Mature human (5)
**19** Regions (5)
**20** Temperature scale (10)
**22** Marine crustaceans (9)
**25** Scowls (7)
**28** Circular in shape (5)
**29** One who makes bread (5)
**30** Dole out (5)
**31** Animal life of a region (5)
**32** Substitute (7)
**34** Advantageous (9)
**36** Separate; distinct (10)
**38** Appear suddenly (3,2)
**40** Steer (anag.) (5)
**43** Large metal pot (8)
**45** Change in appearance (11)
**46** Relating to the south polar region (9)
**47** Scope for freedom (8)
**48** Compelling (11)

## Down

**1** Significant (10)
**2** Leave a place (6)
**3** Denial of something (8)
**4** European country (6)
**5** Ancient or well established (3-3)
**6** Legume (6)
**7** Flatfish (6)
**8** Customary practices (6)
**11** Eyelash cosmetic (7)
**15** Serious (7)
**16** Another option (11)
**17** Unlimited (9)
**18** Vehement denunciations (7)
**21** Meet; come across (9)
**23** Found agreeable (5)
**24** Wander off track (5)
**25** Elegance; class (5)
**26** Spring flower (5)
**27** Least hard (7)
**29** Got on a ship (7)
**33** Possessions (10)
**35** Sum of money put in the bank (7)
**37** Leaping up or over (8)
**38** Flower parts (6)
**39** Puts in the soil (6)
**41** Large birds of prey (6)
**42** Conflict or struggle (6)
**43** Risky (6)
**44** Pull back from (6)

*No. 2*

*No. 3*

## Across

1 Musical film featuring the character Truly Scrumptious (6,6,4,4)
10 Sphere or globe (3)
11 Slow down (5)
14 Lunar features (7)
15 Flower-shaped competition award (7)
16 Uptight (5)
17 Disapproving sound (3)
18 Japanese dish (5)
21 In what way (3)
22 Release someone from duty (7)
23 Expression of approval (13)
25 First woman (3)
27 Pollen traps (anag.) (11)
30 Pertaining to a bishop (9)
31 Respond to (5)
33 The origin of a word (9)
35 Part of (5)
36 Unobserved (9)
38 Substitute (11)
42 Clumsy person (3)
43 Rude and discourteous (13)
45 Tuft of grass (7)
48 Deep anger (3)
49 Respected person in a field (5)
52 Longing (3)
53 Egg-shaped (5)
55 Upper arm bone (7)
56 Cowboy hat (7)
57 In a slow tempo (of music) (5)
58 Draw (3)
59 Film starring Jodie Foster as Clarice Starling (3,7,2,3,5)

## Down

1 Hit hard (7)
2 Very confused situation (9)
3 Scottish national emblem (7)
4 Acrobatic revolution (9)
5 Intermediate (2-7)
6 Wooden crosspiece attached to animals (4)
7 Inevitably (11)
8 Large omnivorous mammals (5)
9 Circumference (5)
12 Loft (5)
13 Speak excitedly of (7)
19 Tall tower (7)
20 Faculty of reasoning (9)
24 Fugitive (7)
26 Immense (4)
27 Talked into doing something (9)
28 Ennoble (7)
29 Track of an animal (5)
32 Official pardon (7)
33 Extraordinary (11)
34 Celebration; festivity (4)
37 Claimed (anag.) (7)
39 Quickly finish something (6,3)
40 Consequences of an event (9)
41 Biological community (9)
44 Entrance hallway (5)
46 Breathing aid in water (7)
47 Shelters for dogs (7)
50 Group of eight (5)
51 Facial protuberances (5)
54 Mineral powder (4)

*No. 3*

*No. 4*

## Across

**10** Not awake (6)
**11** US singer whose hit songs included 'Never Too Much' (6,8)
**12** Plant yield (4)
**13** Personality (9)
**15** More likely than not (4-2)
**16** Pub (3)
**17** Arachnid (6)
**19** Deep fissure (5)
**21** Prosaic; dull (10)
**22** Methodical (10)
**25** Cause friction (3)
**27** Boy (3)
**29** Amongst other things (Latin) (5,4)
**31** Fix (3)
**32** Unidirectional (3-3)
**34** Farewell remark (3)
**35** Large property with land; holding (6)
**36** The gist of the matter (3)
**37** One to whom a letter is directed (9)
**38** Excavated soil (3)
**39** Long-haired ox (3)
**41** Succeed or fail without external help (4,2,4)
**43** In advance (10)
**46** Passage between rows of seats (5)
**48** Exertion (6)
**50** Imitate (3)
**51** Not singular (6)
**53** Obediently (9)
**55** e.g. pecan and cashew (4)
**56** British cyclist and 2012 Tour de France winner (7,7)
**57** Lethargy (6)

## Down

**1** Branch of astronomy (12)
**2** Jumped in the air (6)
**3** Long narrative poem (4)
**4** Neat and smart (5-3)
**5** Capital of Canada (6)
**6** Ate excessively (12)
**7** Recites as a chant (7)
**8** Push; poke (4)
**9** Marriage ceremony (8)
**14** Pack down tightly (4)
**18** Commented (8)
**20** Procedures (9)
**23** Attrition (anag.) (9)
**24** Peevish and annoyed (6)
**26** Brief intervals (6)
**28** Shelter for pigeons (8)
**30** Nocturnal bird of prey (4-5,3)
**33** Improvement in a condition (12)
**40** System by which coats of arms are devised (8)
**42** Unnecessary (8)
**44** Praised highly (7)
**45** Small pointed missile (4)
**47** Element added to the end of a word (6)
**49** Regalia (6)
**52** Travel by horse (4)
**54** Abominable snowman (4)

*No. 4*

1 2 3 4 5 6 7 8 9
10 11
12 13 14 15
16
17 18 19 20
21
22 23 24
25 26 27 28
29 30 31 32 33
34
35 36 37
38 39
40 41 42
43 44 45
46 47 48 49
50
51 52 53 54 55
56 57

*No. 5*

## Across

**9** Accumulates over time (7)
**10** Angry dispute (3-2)
**11** Ploy (6)
**12** One's family (3)
**13** Small tuned drum (5)
**14** Diagrams or pictures (7)
**15** Consented (6)
**16** Observant (8)
**18** Notwithstanding (12)
**20** Removing from the premises (8)
**24** The act of restarting (10)
**27** Put into practice (5)
**28** Molten rock (4)
**30** Not at home (4)
**31** Coal bucket (7)
**32** Regular payment made to a retired person (7)
**33** Days before major events (4)
**34** Utters (4)
**36** Burning (5)
**37** Unprofitable (10)
**38** Explosive (8)
**40** Penny-pinching (12)
**43** Exterior of a motor vehicle (8)
**47** Large military unit (6)
**48** Impressed a pattern on (7)
**49** Inadequately (5)
**50** Legal rule (3)
**51** Sweltering (6)
**52** Frostily (5)
**53** Intrinsic nature (7)

## Down

**1** Country in central Africa (6)
**2** Symbolic (6)
**3** Designated limit (3,3)
**4** Of practical benefit (6)
**5** Shy person (9)
**6** Sink (anag.) (4)
**7** Without ethics (6)
**8** Designed to distract (12)
**10** Revive (10)
**11** Grind together (5)
**16** Round steering device (5)
**17** Head covering (3)
**19** Replied (9)
**21** Traditional example (7)
**22** Pancreatic hormone (7)
**23** Refined males (9)
**25** Model of the body (7)
**26** Crossbar set above a window (7)
**29** Beneficial (12)
**32** Study of the essential nature of reality (10)
**35** Thick slice of meat (5)
**36** Very athletic (9)
**39** Whichever (3)
**41** Very holy people (6)
**42** Virile (5)
**43** Moved (6)
**44** Lower in value (6)
**45** Increases a gap (6)
**46** Poems; sounds alike (6)
**48** Move in water (4)

## No. 5

1 2 3 4 5 6 7 8
9 10 11
12
13 14 15
16 17 18 19
20 21 22 23 24 25 26
27
28 29 30
31 32
33 34 35
36
37 38 39
40 41 42 43 44 45 46
47 48 49
50
51 52 53

*No. 6*

## Across

**1** Trash (6)
**5** Large bodies of water (6)
**8** Platform projecting from a wall (7)
**11** Leap on one foot (3)
**12** Part of a motor (6)
**13** Cosmetic product (9)
**14** Cobras (4)
**15** Formidable (of a person) (11)
**19** Consistently (9)
**20** Profound transformation (3,6)
**22** Following in a logical order (10)
**24** Turmoil (6)
**25** Presupposition (13)
**31** Powerful tractors (10)
**33** Machine with keys (10)
**36** 1965 musical inspired by 'Don Quixote' (3,2,2,6)
**40** Entertained (6)
**42** Undergo; be faced with (10)
**45** Medical analysis (9)
**47** Sickly (9)
**49** Comfort; solace (11)
**53** Inspires fear and wonder (4)
**54** Entry gate (9)
**55** Papal representative (6)
**56** Type of statistical chart (3)
**57** Inscribe (7)
**58** Senior tribal figures (6)
**59** Shows indifference (6)

## Down

**2** Exceptional; not usual (7)
**3** Quantitative relation (5)
**4** Small woody plant (5)
**5** Dramatic musical work (5)
**6** Responses (7)
**7** Current state of affairs (6,3)
**8** Dark red halogen (7)
**9** Device used to go up a mountain (9)
**10** Country in the Himalayas (5)
**16** Unprecedented (7-2)
**17** Makes brown (4)
**18** Short high-pitched tone (5)
**20** Small firework (5)
**21** Fourth month (5)
**23** Not tight (5)
**26** Plant secretion (5)
**27** Receive a ball in one's hands (5)
**28** Sharp bites (4)
**29** Desire to set fire to things (9)
**30** Curl one's hair (4)
**32** Customary practice (5)
**34** Things to be done (5)
**35** Travels on a bicycle (5)
**37** Tyrant (9)
**38** Source of irritation (9)
**39** Supplementary component (3-2)
**41** Part of a pedestal (4)
**43** Trespass (7)
**44** Exhilarated (7)
**46** Smoothing clothes (7)
**48** Certain to fail (2-3)
**50** Paces (5)
**51** Wrinkles in the skin (5)
**52** Singing voice (5)

## No. 6

1 2 3 4 5 6 7 8 9 10
11
12 13 14
15 16 17 18 19
20 21 22 23
24 25 26 27 28 29
30
31 32 33 34 35
36 37 38 39 40
41
42 43 44 45 46
47 48 49 50 51 52
53 54 55
56
57 58 59

## No. 7

### Across

**1** Indie rock band whose songs include 'Dog Days Are Over' (8,3,3,7)
**12** Trembling (9)
**13** Snake (11)
**14** Resistance to change (7)
**15** Lies back lazily in the sun (5)
**16** Strength (5)
**17** Follow the position of (5)
**19** Miserly person (7)
**20** First part of the Bible (3,9)
**22** Con; swindle (4)
**24** Spore-producing organisms (5)
**25** Completely still (10)
**28** Building for gambling (6)
**30** Remains of a fire (5)
**32** Intentionally so written (3)
**33** Higher in place (5)
**35** Young cat (6)
**37** Rattlesnake (10)
**40** Bend (5)
**41** Engrossed (4)
**43** Drawback (12)
**46** Lifting with difficulty (7)
**48** South American animal (5)
**50** Type of leather (5)
**51** Breed of dog (5)
**52** Reticular (7)
**53** Withdrawal of support (11)
**54** Reveries (9)
**55** 1988 comedy film starring Steve Martin and Michael Caine (5,6,10)

### Down

**1** Remains of living things (7)
**2** Symbol of reconciliation (5,6)
**3** Branch of physics (11)
**4** Clematis (anag.) (8)
**5** Long-haired variety of cat (6)
**6** Unit of sound intensity (7)
**7** Mobile phone (7)
**8** Small dust particles (5)
**9** Clan leader (9)
**10** Meddle (9)
**11** Creepiest (7)
**18** Person who writes music (8)
**21** Small in degree (6)
**23** 22nd Greek letter (3)
**24** Grows weary (5)
**25** Small North Atlantic fish (8)
**26** Remove branches (3)
**27** Tennis stroke (5)
**29** Basic metrical unit in a poem (6)
**31** Organ of sight (3)
**33** Not having a written constitution (11)
**34** Take part in (11)
**36** Touch gently (3)
**38** Poor condition (9)
**39** Day of the week (9)
**42** Expression of gratitude (5,3)
**43** Break up (7)
**44** Severe mental suffering (7)
**45** Sparkle (7)
**47** Lubricates (7)
**49** Sour to the taste (6)
**51** Major African river (5)

# No. 7

*No. 8*

## Across

**9** Indescribable (11)
**10** Act of leaving out (8)
**12** Eject diva (anag.) (9)
**13** Defect in the eye (11)
**14** On a higher floor (8)
**16** Messenger (5)
**19** e.g. Wordsworth and Keats (5)
**20** Device to keep a person afloat (4,6)
**22** Making a loud noise (9)
**25** Speak haltingly (7)
**28** Extraterrestrial (5)
**29** Therefore (5)
**30** Attendant upon God (5)
**31** Roman country house (5)
**32** Most poorly lit (7)
**34** Made use of (9)
**36** Sufficiently (10)
**38** Natural elevation (5)
**40** Perspire (5)
**43** Intended to teach (8)
**45** Having a firm basis in reality (11)
**46** Mammal with a pouch (9)
**47** Device that chops up documents (8)
**48** Chance concurrence of events (11)

## Down

**1** Set of four (10)
**2** Weigh up (6)
**3** Roman building (8)
**4** Skips about playfully (6)
**5** Wrestling hold (6)
**6** Gaming tile with pips in each half (6)
**7** Manly (6)
**8** Dwarfish creatures (6)
**11** Hair-cleansing product (7)
**15** Relating to heat (7)
**16** Elaborate; excessive (11)
**17** Inoculate (9)
**18** Longed for (7)
**21** General erudition (9)
**23** Unit of weight (5)
**24** Used up (5)
**25** Tennis stroke (5)
**26** Tool for boring holes (5)
**27** Studies for an exam (7)
**29** Nonconformist (7)
**33** Very tall building (10)
**35** Brought to bear (7)
**37** Support (8)
**38** Oppose (6)
**39** Suspends; prevents (6)
**41** Irrigates (6)
**42** Tips and instruction (6)
**43** Evil spirits (6)
**44** Pressing keys (6)

# *No. 8*

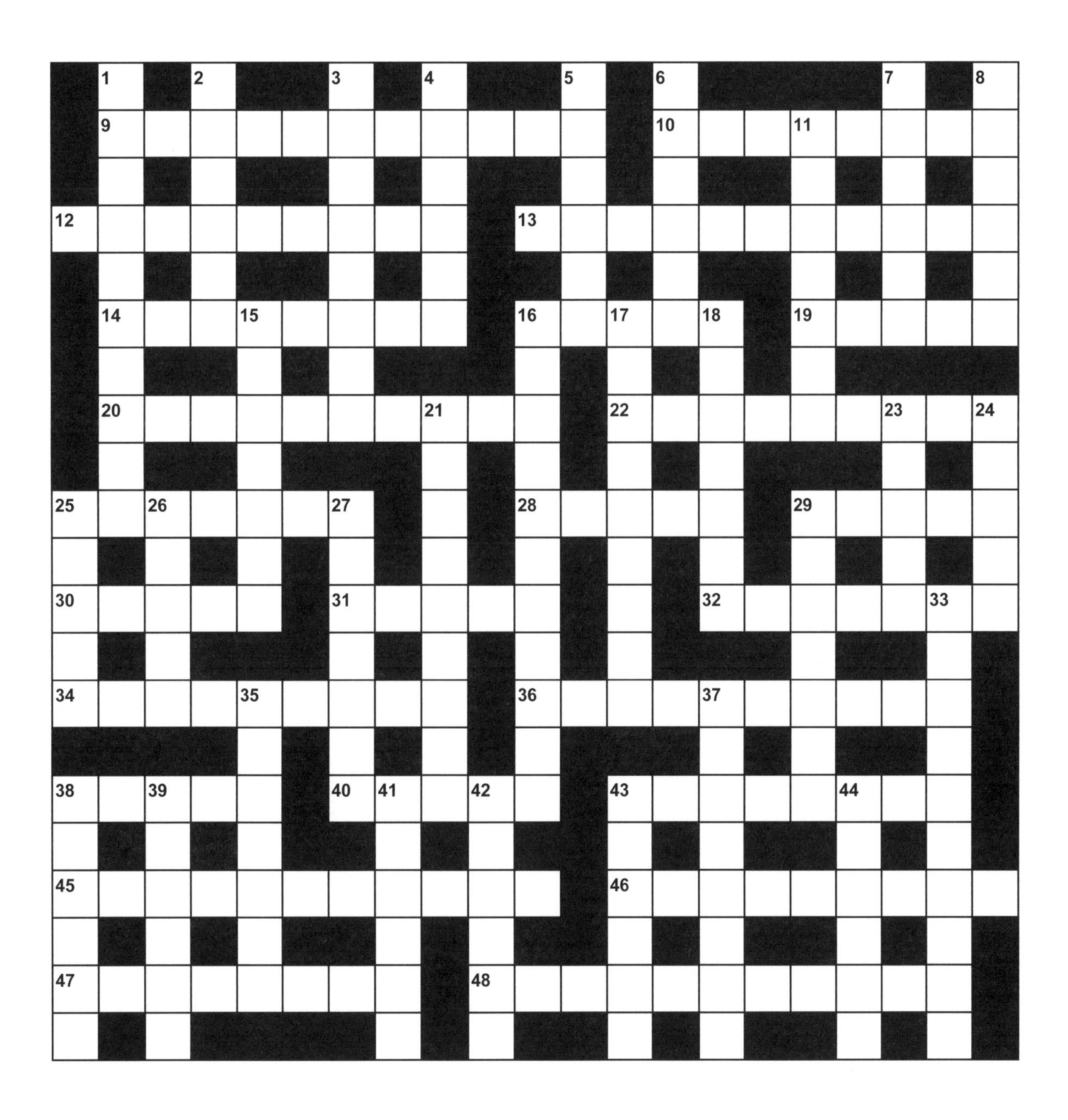

1
2
3
4
5
6
7
8
9
10
11
12
13
14
15
16
17
18
19
20
21
22
23
24
25
26
27
28
29
30
31
32
33
34
35
36
37
38
39
40
41
42
43
44
45
46
47
48

*No. 9*

## Across

**9** Criminal (8)
**11** Not achieving the desired result (11)
**12** Makes better (11)
**13** Signature of a famous person (9)
**14** Loutish person (5)
**15** e.g. spaghetti (5)
**18** Water-resistant jacket (8)
**20** Roman Catholic prelate (9)
**22** Bespoke (of clothes) (6-4)
**24** Compassionate (11)
**26** Unit of electric charge (7)
**29** Settled oneself comfortably (7)
**31** Dizzy (5-6)
**32** How fast one may legally travel (5,5)
**34** Riches (9)
**36** Maritime (8)
**39** Father (5)
**42** Pierced by a sharp object (5)
**45** The people of a country (9)
**46** Large populated area (11)
**47** Brave (11)
**48** The production and discharge of something (8)

## Down

**1** Series of prayers (6)
**2** Anew (6)
**3** Fleet of ships (6)
**4** Process food (6)
**5** Matter (6)
**6** Neutral particle with negligible mass (8)
**7** A size of book page (6)
**8** Current of air near a moving car (10)
**10** Capital of Kenya (7)
**15** Squeezed the skin tightly (7)
**16** Scheme (9)
**17** Hinged; segmented (11)
**19** Calculate (7)
**20** Craftsman who uses stone (5)
**21** Titles (5)
**23** Watered (9)
**25** Illness (7)
**26** e.g. knives and forks (7)
**27** More mature (5)
**28** Remains somewhere (5)
**30** Things that are necessary (10)
**33** Person granted a permit (8)
**35** Gestures that convey meaning (7)
**37** Agreement or concord (6)
**38** Relays (anag.) (6)
**40** Keeps away from (6)
**41** Extinguished (6)
**43** Dried grape (6)
**44** Act of eating out (6)

# No. 9

*No. 10*

## Across

**1** Farm animal (3)
**11** Accord (7)
**12** Sewing instrument (6)
**13** Stagnant; lazy (4)
**14** 24-hour period (3)
**15** War film of 1998 directed by Steven Spielberg (6,7,4)
**16** Passing around a town (of a road) (7)
**18** Unit of weight (3)
**20** Polygon having 12 sides (9)
**22** Eye parts (7)
**24** Relating to vision (5)
**25** Personal possession (7)
**26** Tragedy by Shakespeare (7)
**27** Delicious (11)
**33** Speculative (11)
**36** Not limited to one class (7)
**38** Subatomic particles such as electrons (7)
**40** The prevailing fashion (5)
**41** Chocolate chewy cake (7)
**42** Memorial structures (9)
**44** Dispirited (3)
**46** Betrays (slang) (7)
**48** H. G. Wells novel about Martian invaders (3,3,2,3,6)
**50** Nocturnal mammal (3)
**51** Spoken exam (4)
**52** Oppressively hot (6)
**53** Loaning (7)
**54** Male offspring (3)

## Down

**1** Stiff material made of paper (9)
**2** Dairy product (4)
**3** Adjust in advance of its use (6)
**4** Recovering from illness (of a person) (12)
**5** Young swan (6)
**6** Cut (4)
**7** Recurring at intervals (8)
**8** Lose one's job (3,3,4)
**9** Long mountain chain (6)
**10** Unintelligible (11)
**17** Tar-like hydrocarbon (7)
**19** Memos (5)
**21** Stomach (3)
**23** Shallow recess (5)
**24** Opposite one of two (5)
**28** Scoundrel (5)
**29** Startling (4-8)
**30** Trunk of the body (5)
**31** Elongated rectangles (7)
**32** Enthusiastic approval (11)
**34** Declare sacred (10)
**35** Allowed by official rules (5)
**37** Feeling (9)
**39** Joke (3)
**40** Guests; callers (8)
**43** Ill (6)
**45** Entirely (6)
**47** Attack (6)
**49** Movement of water causing a small whirlpool (4)
**50** Flexible containers (4)

# No. 10

1 2 3 4 5 6 7 8 9 10
11 12 13
14 15
16 17 18 19 20 21
22 23 24 25
26 27 28 29 30 31
32
33 34 35 36
37
38 39 40 41
42 43 44 45 46 47
48 49 50
51 52 53
54

*No. 11*

## Across

**9** Legacy (11)
**10** Puts forward for acceptance (8)
**12** Norms; established criteria (9)
**13** Letter of recommendation (11)
**14** Functioned (8)
**16** Horse carts (5)
**19** Play a guitar (5)
**20** Drug that destroys microorganisms (10)
**22** Happening in fits and starts (9)
**25** Evergreen conifer (7)
**28** Expect (5)
**29** Spirit in a bottle (5)
**30** Individual things (5)
**31** Very masculine (5)
**32** Impressive bird (7)
**34** Maybe (9)
**36** Symptomatic (10)
**38** Ruin (5)
**40** Faithful (5)
**43** Musical pieces for solo instruments (8)
**45** Perilously (11)
**46** Device for catching rodents (9)
**47** Solitary (8)
**48** Unpleasant (11)

## Down

**1** Lexicon (10)
**2** Modify (6)
**3** Opera texts (8)
**4** Stopped temporarily (6)
**5** Shooting star (6)
**6** Having pimples (6)
**7** Creepier (6)
**8** Shelter; place of refuge (6)
**11** Floating wreckage (7)
**15** Plunderers (7)
**16** Autocratic (11)
**17** Refrained from an action (9)
**18** Process of setting something in motion (5-2)
**21** Disloyalty (9)
**23** Wild dog of Australia (5)
**24** Waterway (5)
**25** Small cluster (5)
**26** Earlier (5)
**27** Strongly influencing later developments (7)
**29** Recipient of funding (7)
**33** Commendable (10)
**35** Aides (7)
**37** Be overcome with laughter (8)
**38** Seat on the back of a horse (6)
**39** Possessing (6)
**41** Musical works (6)
**42** Refer to indirectly (6)
**43** Extraterrestrial objects (6)
**44** Give formal consent to (6)

## No. 11

1 2 3 4 5 6 7 8 9 10 11 12 13 14 15 16 17 18 19 20 21 22 23 24 25 26 27 28 29 30 31 32 33 34 35 36 37 38 39 40 41 42 43 44 45 46 47 48

## *No. 12*

### Across

**1** Long speech (6)
**5** Hotter (6)
**8** Shaving of the crown of head (7)
**11** Blade for rowing a boat (3)
**12** Attempting (6)
**13** Barrier around an area (9)
**14** Bucket (4)
**15** Style of painting (8,3)
**19** Translation; a performance (9)
**20** Astonish (9)
**22** Expressing sorrow (10)
**24** Recollection (6)
**25** Pitilessly (13)
**31** Writing materials (10)
**33** Solid figure having ten faces (10)
**36** Reach the required standard (3,3,7)
**40** Averts something bad (6)
**42** Series of links on a web page (10)
**45** Exactly (9)
**47** Very successful performer (9)
**49** Argumentative (11)
**53** Japanese sport (4)
**54** Monarch (9)
**55** In mint condition (6)
**56** Gallivant (3)
**57** Orbs (7)
**58** Stomach crunches (3-3)
**59** Exude (6)

### Down

**2** Reindeer (7)
**3** Declaration (5)
**4** School of thought (5)
**5** Take away by force (5)
**6** Civilians trained as soldiers (7)
**7** Water storage facility (9)
**8** Capital of Ontario (7)
**9** Moves apart (9)
**10** Rule (5)
**16** Renovate; recondition (9)
**17** Successful move (4)
**18** Only poisonous snake in Britain (5)
**20** Concave roofs (5)
**21** Jason ___ : US actor in Aquaman (5)
**23** Stringed instrument (5)
**26** Country in North East Africa (5)
**27** Command (5)
**28** Of like kind (4)
**29** Let oracle (anag.) (9)
**30** Boyfriend or male admirer (4)
**32** Pollex (5)
**34** Take delight in (5)
**35** Beastly (5)
**37** Consequently (9)
**38** Small tree-dwelling rodents (9)
**39** Triangular river mouth (5)
**41** Agitate (4)
**43** Positively charged ions (7)
**44** Legacy (7)
**46** Clinging shellfish (7)
**48** Take the place of (5)
**50** Steps of a ladder (5)
**51** Short musical composition (5)
**52** Mark or wear thin (5)

## No. 12

1 2 3 4 5 6 7 8 9 10
11
12 13 14
15 16 17 18 19
20 21 22 23
24 25 26 27 28 29
30
31 32 33 34 35
36 37 38 39 40
41
42 43 44 45 46
47 48 49 50 51 52
53 54 55
56
57 58 59

## No. 13

### Across

**9** Fast musical composition (7)
**10** Hot fluid rock (5)
**11** Not level (6)
**12** School of Mahayana Buddhism (3)
**13** Got up (5)
**14** Junction between nerve cells (7)
**15** Soldiers (6)
**16** Increase (8)
**18** Lacking courage (5-7)
**20** Region of a shadow (8)
**24** Embroidery (10)
**27** Gives a meal to (5)
**28** Warbled (4)
**30** Pig noise (4)
**31** Lock of curly hair (7)
**32** One who holds property for another (7)
**33** Bone of the forearm (4)
**34** Swerve (4)
**36** Friend (Spanish) (5)
**37** Featureless (of a place) (10)
**38** Channels of the nose (8)
**40** The management of a home (12)
**43** Social gatherings for old friends (8)
**47** Mark of disgrace (6)
**48** Helps to happen (7)
**49** Dried kernel of the coconut (5)
**50** Vessel (3)
**51** Infuriate (6)
**52** Church singers (5)
**53** Expressive (of music) (7)

### Down

**1** Get away from (6)
**2** Crowd (6)
**3** Take into custody (6)
**4** Make less tight (6)
**5** e.g. residents of Cairo (9)
**6** Bewilder; stun (4)
**7** Roundabout route (6)
**8** Re-emergence (12)
**10** Displaying great generosity (10)
**11** Unfasten (5)
**16** Desires (5)
**17** Meat from a pig (3)
**19** Immediately following that (9)
**21** Improve equipment (7)
**22** Large signs (7)
**23** Wealth (9)
**25** Pieces of correspondence sent through the post (7)
**26** Anybody (7)
**29** Crucial (3,9)
**32** Having three corners (10)
**35** Flowers (5)
**36** Semiaquatic reptile (9)
**39** Net (anag.) (3)
**41** Gesture (6)
**42** Rogue; scoundrel (5)
**43** Outcome (6)
**44** Open a wine bottle (6)
**45** Marked effect (6)
**46** Almost (6)
**48** Engrave with acid (4)

## No. 13

1 2 3 4 5 6 7 8
9 10 11
12
13 14 15
16 17 18 19
20 21 22 23 24 25 26
27
28 29 30
31 32
33 34 35
36
37 38 39
40 41 42 43 44 45 46
47 48 49
50
51 52 53

## *No. 14*

### Across

9 Follows (6)
11 Ascend (5)
13 Country in South America (7)
14 Stimulus (3)
15 Domed roof (6)
16 Official sitting (7)
17 Doglike mammal (5)
18 Explanatory (12)
20 Lied under oath (8)
23 Verify with a different method (5-5)
26 Opposite of eastward (8)
29 Apathy (5)
30 Get hold of (6)
31 Lock lips (4)
33 Personal attendant (5)
35 Impersonator (5)
36 Stream or small river (4)
37 Unfold (6)
38 A leaf of paper (5)
40 Not long ago (8)
42 The words of a language (10)
43 In this way; by means of this (8)
48 Failure to act with prudence (12)
51 First Greek letter (5)
52 Certificate (7)
54 Crazy (6)
55 Criticise severely (3)
56 Portable lamp (7)
57 View; picture (5)
58 Annually (6)

### Down

1 Immune (12)
2 Continent (6)
3 Case (anag.) (4)
4 Cosmetics (9)
5 Arrive (4,2)
6 Writer (6)
7 Writing desk (6)
8 Revolve quickly (6)
10 Skin on top of the head (5)
12 Man on his wedding day (10)
19 Illustrate perfectly (9)
21 Extend out (3)
22 Extinct birds (5)
24 Type of fetter (7)
25 Community of nuns (7)
26 Playfully quaint (9)
27 Yield (7)
28 Sleepless (7)
32 Shockingly (12)
34 Items used by astronomers (10)
36 Mooring for a ship (5)
39 Elated (9)
41 At this moment (3)
44 Make possible (6)
45 Increase in size (6)
46 Pictures (6)
47 Concealing (6)
49 Glossy (5)
50 Capital of the Bahamas (6)
53 Summit (4)

*No. 14*

1 2 3 4 5 6 7 8
9 10 11 12 13
14
15 16 17
18 19 20 21 22
23 24 25 26 27 28
29
30 31 32
33 34 35
36 37
38 39
40 41 42
43 44 45 46 47 48 49 50
51 52 53 54
55
56 57 58

## No. 15

### Across

**9** Jobs (11)
**10** Exaggerated emotion (8)
**12** Stances; ways of thinking (9)
**13** Practice of drawing maps (11)
**14** Defensive walls (8)
**16** Purple fruits (5)
**19** Tree of the birch family with toothed leaves (5)
**20** Wind instrument (10)
**22** Prepared in advance (5-4)
**25** e.g. natives of Berlin (7)
**28** Keep cold (11)
**30** Fragility (11)
**31** Pseudoscience (7)
**33** Massive land mammals (9)
**35** Hesitation (10)
**37** Sacred hymn or song (5)
**39** Skirmish (5)
**42** Fraudster (8)
**44** Comradeship (11)
**45** Sailor of a light vessel (9)
**46** First in importance (8)
**47** Fictional (4-7)

### Down

**1** Pedestrian walkway (10)
**2** Division of a group (6)
**3** Person walking aimlessly (8)
**4** Locks lips with (6)
**5** Country in the Middle East (6)
**6** Sense of musical time (6)
**7** Covered in cloth (6)
**8** Woodcutter (6)
**11** Having three sections (7)
**15** Costumed procession (7)
**16** Happening in stages (11)
**17** Coarse (9)
**18** Endurance (7)
**21** Process of scattering (9)
**23** With speed (5)
**24** Military opponent (5)
**25** Triangular wall part (5)
**26** Lift up (5)
**27** Breastbone (7)
**29** Released from a duty (7)
**32** One who knows your thoughts (4,6)
**34** Boring (7)
**36** Conclusive argument (8)
**37** Appease (6)
**38** Regard with approval (6)
**40** Expels (6)
**41** Complex problem (6)
**42** Fashioned (6)
**43** Inferior (6)

# No. 15

*No. 16*

## Across

**9** Monist (anag.) (6)
**11** Effigies (5)
**13** Study of the body (7)
**14** Piece of cloth (3)
**15** Instrumental piece of music (6)
**16** Not artificial (7)
**17** Italian cathedral (5)
**18** Reclamation (12)
**20** Locate exactly (8)
**23** From now on (10)
**26** Lower (8)
**29** Store of hoarded wealth (5)
**30** Walk casually (6)
**31** A single time (4)
**33** Dispose of (5)
**35** Not wet (3)
**36** Stringed instrument (4)
**37** Extraterrestrials (6)
**38** Rides the waves (5)
**40** Fabric strips for covering wounds (8)
**42** Having three sides (10)
**43** Reasoning logically (8)
**48** Carefree (5-2-5)
**51** Reduce the temperature of (5)
**52** Largest anthropoid ape (7)
**54** Thin candles (6)
**55** Compete for (3)
**56** Active during the day (7)
**57** Espresso coffee and steamed milk (5)
**58** Regain (6)

## Down

**1** Incomprehensibly (12)
**2** Red salad fruit (6)
**3** Indication (4)
**4** Period of two weeks (9)
**5** Beat soundly (6)
**6** Make unhappy (6)
**7** Excessively ornate (of music) (6)
**8** Wealthy person in business (6)
**10** Shallow food containers (5)
**12** Fortress (10)
**19** Witch (9)
**21** For each (3)
**22** At that place; not here (5)
**24** Small storage rooms or cupboards (7)
**25** Copious (7)
**26** Explain or clarify (9)
**27** Plant with starchy tuberous roots (7)
**28** Passionate (7)
**32** Quarrelsome and uncooperative (12)
**34** Situated on the edge of something (10)
**36** Oily organic compound (5)
**39** Specify a condition (9)
**41** Involuntary spasm (3)
**44** Encrypt (6)
**45** One of a kind (6)
**46** Land surrounded by water (6)
**47** Flock of geese (6)
**49** External (5)
**50** Remove from a container (6)
**53** Affirm with confidence (4)

## No. 17

### Across

**10** Single-celled organism (6)
**11** Puerto Rican actor in 'The Usual Suspects' (7,3,4)
**12** Statistics and facts (4)
**13** Breaks into pieces (9)
**15** State of sleep (6)
**16** Frozen water (3)
**17** Current of air (6)
**19** Arm of a body of water (5)
**21** In all places (10)
**22** Mechanism in a clock (10)
**25** Tear (3)
**27** Help; assist (3)
**29** Inducement (9)
**31** Mock (3)
**32** Within a space (6)
**34** Sound of a cow (3)
**35** Arctic abodes (6)
**36** Before the present (of time) (3)
**37** State of poverty (9)
**38** Sorrowful (3)
**39** Mud channel (3)
**41** Burdening (10)
**43** Branch of linguistics (10)
**46** Became less difficult (5)
**48** Go from one place to another (6)
**50** Absolutely (3)
**51** Crown (6)
**53** Encroaches on (9)
**55** Pal (4)
**56** Progressive (7-7)
**57** Mineral used to make plaster of Paris (6)

### Down

**1** Awkward (12)
**2** Recreate (6)
**3** Stick with a hook (4)
**4** Grammatical case (8)
**5** Type of living organism (6)
**6** Significant (12)
**7** Furtiveness (7)
**8** Finish (4)
**9** Kitchen sideboards (8)
**14** Short letter (4)
**18** Fairness (8)
**20** Farm machines (9)
**23** Action of securing something to a base (9)
**24** Quiver (6)
**26** Quickly (6)
**28** Industrious (8)
**30** Not allowable (12)
**33** Insincere (12)
**40** Qualifications (8)
**42** Method and practice of teaching (8)
**44** From now on (7)
**45** A person's individuality (4)
**47** Ghost (6)
**49** Consider to be true (6)
**52** Opposite of up (4)
**54** Wise; herb (4)

## No. 17

1 2 3 4 5 6 7 8 9
10 11
12 13 14 15
16
17 18 19 20
21
22 23 24
25 26 27 28
29 30 31 32 33
34
35 36 37
38 39
40 41 42
43 44 45
46 47 48 49
50
51 52 53 54 55
56 57

## No. 18

### Across

**9** Amino acid (7)
**10** Trims (5)
**11** Ordered arrangements (6)
**12** Ignited (3)
**13** e.g. an Oscar or Grammy (5)
**14** Pear-shaped fruit native to Mexico (7)
**15** Isolated inlet of the sea (6)
**16** Fibrous connective tissue (8)
**18** Educational institutions (12)
**20** Weapon (8)
**24** Society governed by women (10)
**27** Goodbye (Spanish) (5)
**28** e.g. an arm or leg (4)
**30** Flashing point on a radar screen (4)
**31** Accept to be true (7)
**32** Burnt (7)
**33** Volcano in Sicily (4)
**34** Expel; drive out (4)
**36** Greeting (5)
**37** Causing irritation (10)
**38** Evoke memories (8)
**40** Person who receives office visitors (12)
**43** Damage (a reputation) (8)
**47** Agreement (6)
**48** Garden bird (7)
**49** Type of sweet (5)
**50** One and one (3)
**51** Garrulous; insolent (6)
**52** Iron alloy (5)
**53** Apprehensive (7)

### Down

**1** Italian sausage (6)
**2** Where one finds Quebec (6)
**3** Start a fire (6)
**4** Occupant (6)
**5** Living things (9)
**6** Capital of Norway (4)
**7** Radiating light; clever (6)
**8** Firework display (12)
**10** Fruitful (10)
**11** Collection of maps (5)
**16** In the area (5)
**17** Title of a married woman (3)
**19** Most irate (anag.) (9)
**21** Day of rest (7)
**22** Large rock (7)
**23** Sport played in a pool (5,4)
**25** Traditional piano keys (7)
**26** e.g. use a towel after showering (3-4)
**29** Shyness (12)
**32** Security for a loan (10)
**35** e.g. incisors and molars (5)
**36** Equivocated (9)
**39** Unit of resistance (3)
**41** Constructs; builds (6)
**42** Tawdry (5)
**43** Lowering one's head to show respect (6)
**44** Sightseeing trip in Africa (6)
**45** Situated within a building (6)
**46** Dairy product (6)
**48** Mediocre (2-2)

## *No. 18*

1 2 3 4 5 6 7 8
9 10 11
12
13 14 15
16 17 18 19
20 21 22 23 24 25 26
27
28 29 30
31 32
33 34 35
36
37 38 39
40 41 42 43 44 45 46
47 48 49
50
51 52 53

*No. 19*

## Across

**9** At any time (8)
**11** In an abundant and lush manner (11)
**12** Causing difficulties (11)
**13** Pirate (9)
**14** Fault; mistake (5)
**15** Theme for a discussion (5)
**18** Stiff coarse hairs (8)
**20** Actor (9)
**22** State of the USA (10)
**24** Camaraderie (11)
**26** Begged (7)
**29** Designer of trendy clothes (7)
**31** Beyond acceptability (3,2,6)
**32** Resort in Monaco (5,5)
**34** Layer of cells covering an organism (9)
**36** Aromatic herb (8)
**39** Small branch (5)
**42** Male bee (5)
**45** Numerical fact (9)
**46** Forever (2,9)
**47** Pretentious display (11)
**48** Re-evaluate (8)

## Down

**1** Bandage (6)
**2** Eat hungrily; gobble (6)
**3** Wall painting; mural (6)
**4** Former students (6)
**5** Confused noise (6)
**6** Devilry (8)
**7** Not written in any key (of music) (6)
**8** The online world (10)
**10** Import barrier (7)
**15** Storm (7)
**16** Buyer (9)
**17** Producing a discordant mix of sounds (11)
**19** Submarine weapon (7)
**20** Chooses (5)
**21** Card game (5)
**23** Unit of astronomical length (5,4)
**25** Pilot (7)
**26** Panting (7)
**27** Fabric used to make jeans (5)
**28** Cleans (5)
**30** Desire to do something (10)
**33** Consider carefully (8)
**35** Final parts of stories (7)
**37** Revolve (6)
**38** Subtle detail (6)
**40** One overly concerned with minor details (6)
**41** Refuse to acknowledge (6)
**43** Beginning (6)
**44** Entangle (6)

## No. 19

1 2 3 4 5 6 7 8
9 10 11
12 13
14 15 16 17 18 19
20 21 22 23
24 25 26 27 28
29 30 31
32 33 34 35
36 37 38 39 40 41 42 43 44
45 46
47 48

*No. 20*

## Across

9 Clay pottery (11)
10 Observing (8)
12 Pennants (9)
13 Fear of open spaces (11)
14 Written agreements (8)
16 Military trainee (5)
19 Correct (5)
20 Sprite of Irish folklore (10)
22 Living things (9)
25 Reveal (7)
28 Unbuttoned (5)
29 Large American felines (5)
30 Brushed clean (5)
31 Muscular contraction (5)
32 Blissful state (7)
34 Cyclones (9)
36 Certain to happen (10)
38 Songbird (5)
40 Criminal (5)
43 Vindictive (8)
45 Revive (11)
46 Herbaceous Caribbean plant (9)
47 Wealth (8)
48 Preference; liking (11)

## Down

1 Athletics contest (10)
2 Turn to ice (6)
3 Large root vegetable (8)
4 Distorts (6)
5 Figure of speech (6)
6 False (6)
7 Safety device in a car (6)
8 Struck by overwhelming shock (6)
11 Acquire from a relative (7)
15 Flight hub (7)
16 The using up of a resource (11)
17 Moral decline; self-indulgence (9)
18 Foot pedal (7)
21 Assessment or evaluation (9)
23 Cuban folk dance (5)
24 Impudent; full of spirit (5)
25 Surprise result (5)
26 Make less miserable (5)
27 Start (4,3)
29 Corridor (7)
33 Enchanted (10)
35 A dancer or singer (7)
37 Lacking knowledge (8)
38 Tropical bird (6)
39 Show-off (6)
41 One or the other of two (6)
42 Deceive with ingenuity (6)
43 Feasible (6)
44 Disallow; prevent (6)

*No. 20*

1 2 3 4 5 6 7 8
9 10 11
12 13
14 15 16 17 18 19
20 21 22 23 24
25 26 27 28 29
30 31 32 33
34 35 36 37
38 39 40 41 42 43 44
45 46
47 48

*No. 21*

## Across

**1** Housing (6)
**4** Children's book by Craig Smith (3,5,6)
**10** Relating to the kidneys (5)
**13** Callous (11)
**15** Go back on (7)
**17** Lacking confidence (8)
**19** Disease (8)
**20** Become less intense (5)
**23** Measure of heat (11)
**25** Joins together (6)
**26** Disgusting (4)
**28** Senior figure in a tribe (5)
**29** Two-horned large African mammal (5,10)
**32** Tilt to one side (4)
**34** Departs (4)
**36** Not well (5,3,7)
**40** Supply with new weapons (5)
**41** Too; in addition (4)
**42** True skin (6)
**43** Shade of blue (11)
**46** Took illegally (5)
**48** Repugnance (8)
**49** Altruistic (8)
**51** Time between events (7)
**53** These are put up at Christmas (11)
**55** Gave away (5)
**58** Author of the 'Alex Cross' series of novels (5,9)
**59** Lacking the skill to do something (6)

## Down

**1** Aggressive dog (3)
**2** What our planet orbits (3)
**3** Longest river (4)
**4** Dictatorial (12)
**5** Limiest (anag.) (7)
**6** Fertile spot in a desert (5)
**7** Range of knowledge (3)
**8** Last longer than others (of clothes) (7)
**9** Small hole (6)
**11** Outer (8)
**12** Creative (8)
**14** Coal containers (8)
**16** Finance department (8)
**18** Breadwinner (6)
**21** Tool for marking angles (5)
**22** Voter (7)
**24** Forerunner (9)
**27** Nationality of Oscar Wilde (5)
**29** Mendicants (7)
**30** e.g. maples and sycamores (5)
**31** Excessive response (12)
**33** e.g. hats and helmets (8)
**35** Capital of South Korea (5)
**36** Portable device to keep rain out (8)
**37** Dreary (6)
**38** Wearisome (8)
**39** Concluding section (8)
**44** Periods of instruction (7)
**45** Demands forcefully (7)
**47** Frozen plain (6)
**50** Run away with a lover (5)
**52** Small symbol or graphic (4)
**54** Exclamation of contempt (3)
**56** Give a nickname to (3)
**57** Female kangaroo (3)

# No. 21

1 2 3 4 5 6 7 8 9
10 11 12 13 14
15 16
17 18
19 20 21 22
23 24
25 26 27
28
29 30 31 32
33
34 35 36 37 38 39
40
41 42
43 44 45
46 47 48
49 50
51 52
53 54 55 56 57
58 59

## No. 22

### Across

**9** Keyboard instrument (11)
**10** Gather together and merge (8)
**12** Person chosen for a job (9)
**13** Book issued for sale (11)
**14** A canine (3,5)
**16** Rushes (5)
**19** Extremely happy period (5)
**20** Strong support for one's country (10)
**22** Having a practical point of view (9)
**25** Adult (5-2)
**28** Hostility (11)
**30** Narrator (11)
**31** Brave and persistent (7)
**33** Suctioned (anag.) (9)
**35** Sensible (2-8)
**37** Period of keeping awake to pray (5)
**39** In what place (5)
**42** Grow; sprout (8)
**44** Daring (11)
**45** Deficit in a bank account (9)
**46** Start (8)
**47** Examine in detail (11)

### Down

**1** Owner of a retail store (10)
**2** Bird with yellow and black plumage (6)
**3** Person highly skilled in music (8)
**4** Beat as if with a flail (6)
**5** Request earnestly (6)
**6** Climbed (6)
**7** Scarcity (6)
**8** Shelter for a dog (6)
**11** Radioactive element (7)
**15** Cruel use of authority (7)
**16** A recollection (11)
**17** Act of removal (9)
**18** Deprived of food (7)
**21** Impertinence (9)
**23** Freshwater fish (5)
**24** Requiring much mastication (5)
**25** e.g. oxygen and nitrogen (5)
**26** Egg-shaped solid (5)
**27** Trailer (7)
**29** Noisiest (7)
**32** Subsequently (10)
**34** Conspire to commit a fraud (7)
**36** Disregards (8)
**37** In a lively manner (6)
**38** Set of chromosomes (6)
**40** Makes a sibilant sound (6)
**41** Continue to exist (6)
**42** Plant with deep purple flowers (6)
**43** Pilot (6)

# No. 22

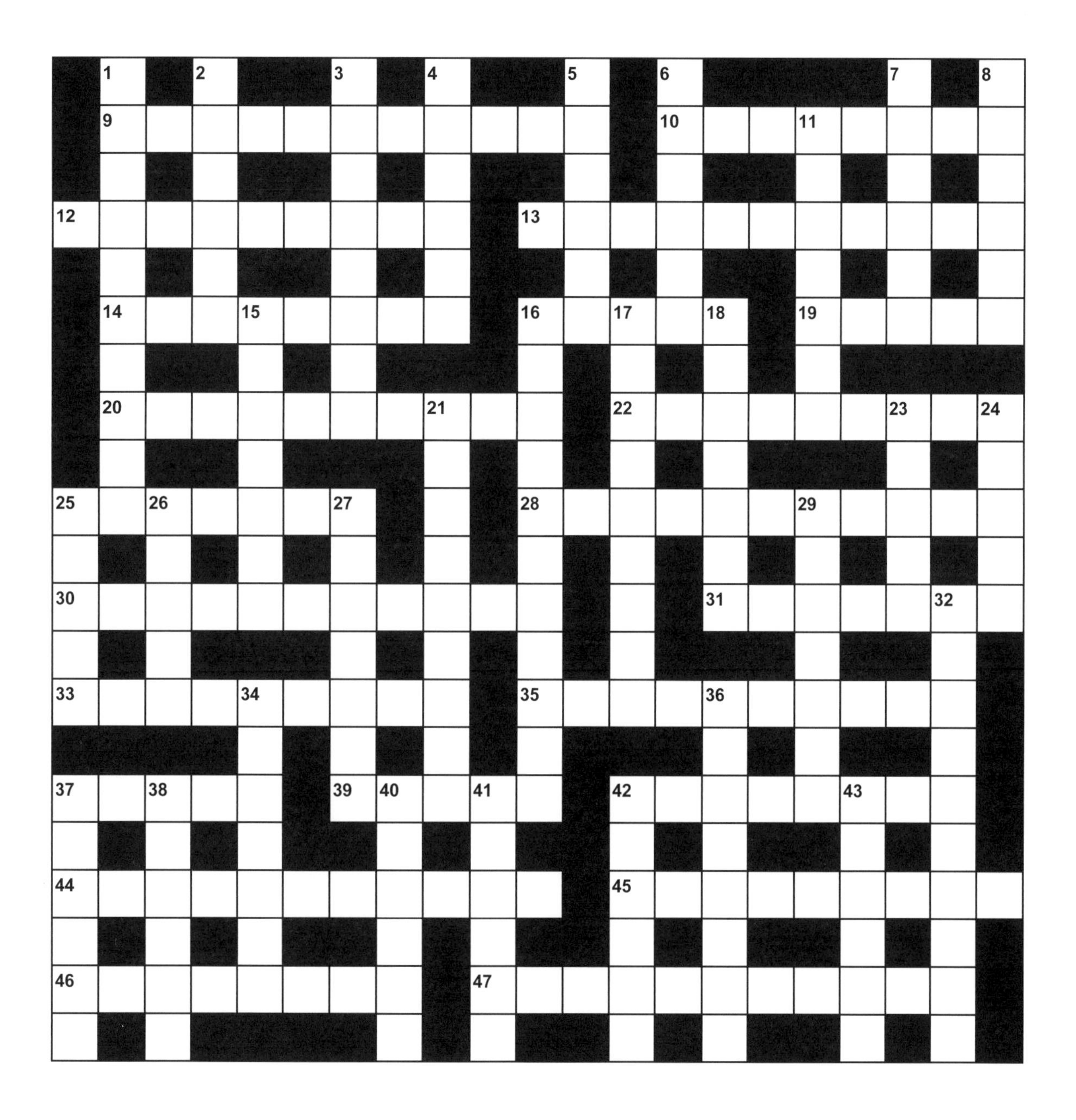

*No. 23*

## Across

**9** The scholastic world (8)
**11** Group of islands (11)
**12** Re-evaluation (11)
**13** Female writer (9)
**14** Insect grub (5)
**15** Staple (5)
**18** Thing serving as an appropriate model (8)
**20** Record of events (9)
**22** Creamy mist (anag.) (10)
**24** Wholehearted (4-7)
**26** Most profound (7)
**29** Timidness (7)
**31** Replaced with another (11)
**32** Last monarch of the House of Tudor (9,1)
**34** Contributions (9)
**36** Subsidiary (8)
**39** Supporting frame used by an artist (5)
**42** Semiconductor (5)
**45** Church minister (9)
**46** Thinking about (11)
**47** Ghost (11)
**48** Living (8)

## Down

**1** Shrub with glossy leaves (6)
**2** Type of market (6)
**3** Capital of the Philippines (6)
**4** US state of islands (6)
**5** Saying (6)
**6** Against the current (8)
**7** Keep watch over an area (6)
**8** Builds; assembles (10)
**10** Give reasons for (7)
**15** Summons with the hand (7)
**16** Quickest (9)
**17** Stealthy (11)
**19** Not in a hurry (7)
**20** Eateries (5)
**21** Exchange of tennis strokes (5)
**23** Annuals (9)
**25** Zephyrs (7)
**26** Obedient (7)
**27** Consumed (of food) (5)
**28** Ocean movements (5)
**30** Secret symbol (10)
**33** Item used to remember the page you're on (8)
**35** Symptom of blushing (7)
**37** Resolutely (6)
**38** Christmas decoration (6)
**40** Long-legged rodent (6)
**41** Christian festival (6)
**43** Egyptian god (6)
**44** Hire for work (6)

*No. 23*

## No. 24

### Across

**1** US actor who won an Oscar for his role in 'Capote' (6,7,7)
**10** Droop (3)
**11** Brown earth pigment (5)
**14** Uppermost layer of something (7)
**15** Learn new skills (7)
**16** Draw or bring out (5)
**17** Popular beverage (3)
**18** Pulsate (5)
**21** Owns (3)
**22** Genuine (7)
**23** Unpredictable (13)
**25** Affirmative vote (3)
**27** Easily made angry (3-8)
**30** Driving sand or snow (9)
**31** Acer tree (5)
**33** Medical practitioner (9)
**35** Keen (5)
**36** Citadel at Athens (9)
**38** Suspicious (11)
**42** Small legume (3)
**43** Hidden store of valuables (8,5)
**45** Waterfall (7)
**48** Large deer (3)
**49** Enclosed (5)
**52** Opposite of cold (3)
**53** Vast multitude (5)
**55** Large household water container (7)
**56** Contentedly (7)
**57** Fight (3-2)
**58** Pot (3)
**59** Children's book by Beatrix Potter (3,4,2,5,6)

### Down

**1** Old Spanish currency (pl.) (7)
**2** Firmly established (9)
**3** Form of an element (7)
**4** Pile of refuse (9)
**5** Child (9)
**6** Not new (4)
**7** Remark; comment (11)
**8** Top degree mark (5)
**9** Tortilla topped with cheese (5)
**12** Darken (5)
**13** Competitors in a sprint (7)
**19** Decaying (7)
**20** Having two sides (9)
**24** Interminable (7)
**26** Loud cry (4)
**27** Using extravagant language (9)
**28** Frees from an obligation (7)
**29** Removed water (5)
**32** Packages (7)
**33** Green pigment in plants (11)
**34** Poker stake (4)
**37** Easy shots (in sport) (7)
**39** Watercraft with a motor (9)
**40** Fraudster (9)
**41** Source of a brief burst of bright light (9)
**44** Start of (5)
**46** Kitchen implement (7)
**47** No longer in existence (7)
**50** Separated (5)
**51** Wander aimlessly (5)
**54** Unable to hear (4)

## *No. 24*

1 2 3 4 5 6 7 8 9
10 11 12 13 14
15 16
17 18 19 20
21
22 23 24
25 26
27 28 29 30
31 32 33 34 35
36 37 38 39 40 41
42
43 44 45 46 47
48
49 50 51 52
53 54 55
56 57 58
59

*No. 25*

## Across

**1** Former Greek monetary unit (7)
**5** Half-conscious state (6)
**8** Frames used by artists (6)
**11** Lively dance (3)
**12** Bristle (4)
**13** Sensible (9)
**14** Races with batons (6)
**15** Deserted settlement (5,4)
**16** Poverty (11)
**20** Consent (10)
**21** Postponement (9)
**24** US artist and member of the Pop Art movement (3,10)
**29** Reason for doing something (6)
**31** Type of rabbit (10)
**33** Roughness (of water) (10)
**35** Street (6)
**36** Untiring (13)
**40** Person bringing a legal case (9)
**42** Personal timepiece (5,5)
**44** Type of social occasion (6,5)
**48** Pecking order (9)
**50** Daniel (anag.) (6)
**51** Decorations (9)
**52** Resistance units (4)
**53** Small sprite (3)
**54** Book of the Bible (6)
**55** Buys and sells goods (6)
**56** Distinguished (7)

## Down

**2** Arrive at (5)
**3** Bottle opener (9)
**4** Laborious (7)
**5** Occurring every three years (9)
**6** Desert (7)
**7** Dismiss from office (5)
**8** White waterbird (5)
**9** Divide; separate (5)
**10** Give up or surrender something (3,4)
**17** Country in North East Africa (5)
**18** Doubtful (4)
**19** Pulling out of the ground (9)
**20** Camera image (5)
**22** Expel from a country (5)
**23** Youngsters aged from 13 - 19 (5)
**25** Fluent use of language (9)
**26** School test (4)
**27** Large fruit with pulpy flesh (5)
**28** Mother-of-pearl (5)
**30** Soft drink (US) (4)
**31** Grasp tightly (5)
**32** Eighth Greek letter (5)
**34** Spirit of the air (5)
**36** Conclude (5)
**37** Scares (9)
**38** This follows morning (9)
**39** Speech impediment (4)
**41** Stands about idly (7)
**42** Capricious; difficult to control (7)
**43** Table support (7)
**45** Horse sound (5)
**46** Measuring stick (5)
**47** High up (5)
**49** Mortal (5)

## No. 25

## *No. 26*

### Across

**9** Praiseworthy (11)
**10** Large retail store (8)
**12** Lying down (9)
**13** Endorsed (11)
**14** Expulsion (8)
**16** Lacking enthusiasm; weary (5)
**19** Mix up or confuse (5)
**20** Assigning (10)
**22** Stood by; provided encouragement (9)
**25** Challenging (7)
**28** Eternal (11)
**30** Company (11)
**31** Form of speech specific to a region (7)
**33** Exploding star (9)
**35** Hostile (10)
**37** Device for sharpening razors (5)
**39** Chasm (5)
**42** Viewing (8)
**44** Data (11)
**45** Cultivation of plants (9)
**46** Wood preserver (8)
**47** Very charming (11)

### Down

**1** Increase speed (10)
**2** Resistant to something (6)
**3** Aromatic plant used in cooking (8)
**4** Move or travel hurriedly (6)
**5** Swiss city (6)
**6** Extract meaning from (6)
**7** Out of breath (6)
**8** Smear or blur (6)
**11** Perennial herb (7)
**15** Spicy Spanish sausage (7)
**16** Large and heavy vehicles (11)
**17** Incredulity (9)
**18** Mottled (7)
**21** Not real (9)
**23** Social division in some societies (5)
**24** A finger or toe (5)
**25** Parasitic arachnids (5)
**26** Remove paint from a wall (5)
**27** Kind of breakfast cereal (7)
**29** Steadfast (7)
**32** Branch of physics (10)
**34** Gives an account of (7)
**36** Intrigue (8)
**37** Pain in the side (6)
**38** Roof beam (6)
**40** Superior (6)
**41** Sear (6)
**42** Gambles (6)
**43** Inborn (6)

## *No. 26*

1 2 3 4 5 6 7 8
9 10 11
12 13
14 15 16 17 18 19
20 21 22 23 24
25 26 27 28 29
30 31 32
33 34 35 36
37 38 39 40 41 42 43
44 45
46 47

## No. 27

### Across

**1** Accept without protest (9)
**6** Painting medium (7)
**10** Canine (3)
**12** Song performed by Kenny Rogers and Dolly Parton (7,2,3,6)
**13** Decorated a cake (4)
**14** Branch of knowledge (9)
**16** Lengthen (8)
**17** After the beginning of (4)
**18** Insults (11)
**21** Elf or fairy (6)
**23** Opposite of bottom (3)
**25** Musical composition (7)
**27** Small stall at a fair (8)
**29** Mathematically aware (8)
**30** Reserved and shy (7)
**31** Engravings (8)
**33** Encrypting (8)
**35** Taught (7)
**38** Drowned river valley (3)
**39** Relaxed and informal (6)
**40** Retail nerve (anag.) (11)
**42** Adjoin (4)
**44** Unidentified (8)
**46** Tourist (9)
**48** Whirring sound (4)
**49** Song by the rock band the Police (5,6,3,4)
**51** Fluffy scarf (3)
**52** Affinity (7)
**53** Puts at risk (9)

### Down

**1** Descend down a rock face (6)
**2** Strict isolation (10)
**3** Signal (8)
**4** Slid (7)
**5** Not part of the essential nature of a thing (9)
**6** Golf peg (3)
**7** Saying; slogan (5)
**8** Mournful poem (5)
**9** Give or apply (a remedy) (10)
**11** Person invited to one's house (5)
**15** Last Greek letter (5)
**19** Mapped out in advance (7)
**20** Of the universe (6)
**22** Indicator (7)
**24** Garden flower (7)
**25** Tornado (7)
**26** Freight (5)
**28** History play by Shakespeare (5,1)
**32** Great distress (10)
**34** Make angry (10)
**36** Religious doctrine (5)
**37** Repeat (9)
**39** Loss of importance or status (8)
**41** Staggered (7)
**43** Promotional wording (5)
**45** Calls to mind (6)
**46** Hank of wool (5)
**47** Sculptured symbol (5)
**50** Knock vigorously (3)

## No. 27

1 2 3 4 5 6 7 8 9 10 11 12 13 14 15 16 17 18 19 20 21 22 23 24 25 26 27 28 29 30 31 32 33 34 35 36 37 38 39 40 41 42 43 44 45 46 47 48 49 50 51 52 53

## *No. 28*

### Across

**9** Refreshing drink (6,5)
**10** Intrusive (8)
**12** Month (9)
**13** Unwilling (11)
**14** Easily frightened (8)
**16** First appearance (5)
**19** Movable helmet part (5)
**20** Suited for land and water (10)
**22** Do in turn repeatedly (9)
**25** Majestically (7)
**28** Suggesting indirectly (11)
**30** Curative (11)
**31** Consume by fire (7)
**33** Quantity that is left over (9)
**35** Unable to count (10)
**37** Water container (5)
**39** Sowed (anag.) (5)
**42** Send to a different place (8)
**44** Rural scenery (11)
**45** Where water meets land (9)
**46** Wanders at random (8)
**47** Detailed examination (11)

### Down

**1** Increase the power of (10)
**2** Small chicken (6)
**3** Assimilate again (8)
**4** Excessive self-confidence (6)
**5** State the meaning of (6)
**6** One's environment (6)
**7** Wicked people (6)
**8** Transmitter (6)
**11** Finished (3,4)
**15** Character in Hamlet (7)
**16** Noticeably different (11)
**17** Ship's officer (9)
**18** Of great size (7)
**21** Depose (9)
**23** Word of farewell (5)
**24** Number after seven (5)
**25** Armature of an electric motor (5)
**26** Shine brightly (5)
**27** Gave way to pressure (7)
**29** Suitor (7)
**32** Making more palatable (10)
**34** Caused to burn (7)
**36** Barely adequate (8)
**37** Developed into (6)
**38** Sharp shrill cry (6)
**40** Be preoccupied with something (6)
**41** Saturated with liquid (6)
**42** Steal livestock (6)
**43** Cream pastry (6)

## No. 28

## No. 29

### Across

**1** Rough (of water) (6)
**4** Part of a building above its foundations (14)
**10** Academy award (5)
**13** Direction (11)
**15** Chatter on and on (7)
**17** Cleansed thoroughly (8)
**19** More powerful (8)
**20** Go in (5)
**23** Adequate in number (11)
**25** Minimal bathing suit (6)
**26** Enclose in paper (4)
**28** Fill with high spirits (5)
**29** Third US President and Founding Father (6,9)
**32** Metal fastener (4)
**34** Lower limbs (4)
**36** 1955 song made popular by the Righteous Brothers (9,6)
**40** Negatively charged ion (5)
**41** One less than ten (4)
**42** Push forcefully (6)
**43** Daring; bold (11)
**46** Add coal to a fire (5)
**48** Walked unsteadily (8)
**49** Obviously offensive (of an action) (8)
**51** Respects (7)
**53** Attention-grabbing (3-8)
**55** Rejuvenate (5)
**58** Offset (14)
**59** Functional (6)

### Down

**1** Dove sound (3)
**2** Monstrous humanoid creature (3)
**3** Cat sound (4)
**4** Underground (12)
**5** Clergymen (7)
**6** Vertical part of a step (5)
**7** Rocky peak (3)
**8** Stronghold (7)
**9** Go back on (6)
**11** Playful (8)
**12** Pithy saying (8)
**14** Undefeated (8)
**16** Most annoyed (8)
**18** Male relatives (6)
**21** Amphibians (5)
**22** Quickly (7)
**24** Device that stimulates the heart muscle (9)
**27** Imitative of the past (5)
**29** Skills (7)
**30** Musical instrument (5)
**31** Make a guess that is too high (12)
**33** Copycat (8)
**35** Go stealthily or furtively (5)
**36** Play a role with great restraint (8)
**37** Depression from a meteor impact (6)
**38** Gift of money (8)
**39** Distribute (8)
**44** Excess of liabilities over assets (7)
**45** Eight-sided polygon (7)
**47** Dinner jacket (6)
**50** A satellite of Uranus (5)
**52** Long periods of history (4)
**54** Taxi (3)
**56** Arrest; apprehend (3)
**57** Great sorrow (3)

No. 29

1 2 3 4 5 6 7 8 9
10 11 12 13 14
15 16
17 18
19 20 21 22
23 24
25 26 27
28
29 30 31 32
33
34 35 36 37 38 39
40
41 42
43 44 45
46 47 48
49 50
51 52
53 54 55 56 57
58 59

## *No. 30*

### Across

9 Vessels for boiling water (7)
10 Piece of code to automate a task (5)
11 Admit openly (6)
12 Large (3)
13 Damp (5)
14 Takes a firm stand (7)
15 Impose or require (6)
16 Certain to fail (8)
18 Establish as genuine (12)
20 Restful (8)
24 Mandatory (10)
27 Cloth woven from flax (5)
28 Sixth Greek letter (4)
30 Cereal grains (4)
31 Quickly (7)
32 Urged on (7)
33 Skin irritation (4)
34 Mud (4)
36 Mournful song (5)
37 Intrusive and interfering (10)
38 Loss of hearing (8)
40 Forcible indoctrination (12)
43 Type of crime (8)
47 Machine that produces motion (6)
48 Satisfy (7)
49 Scraped at (5)
50 Young dog (3)
51 Expenditure (6)
52 Basic units of an element (5)
53 Secret affair (7)

### Down

1 With hands on the hips (6)
2 Hit hard (6)
3 Dress (6)
4 Academy Awards (6)
5 Growth by gradual accumulation (9)
6 Steals from (4)
7 Written in verse (6)
8 Author of screenplays (12)
10 Erroneously (10)
11 Representative (5)
16 SI unit of frequency (5)
17 Illumination unit (3)
19 Brightened up (9)
21 Feeling embarrassed (7)
22 Encroach (7)
23 Sticky (9)
25 State of the USA (7)
26 Walked upon (7)
29 Someone who sets up their own business (12)
32 Woodwind instrument (3,7)
35 Delicious (5)
36 Divergence from a course (9)
39 Pear-shaped fruit (3)
41 Frozen water spear (6)
42 Tearful (5)
43 Insect of the order Coleoptera (6)
44 Revoke a law (6)
45 Opposite of highest (6)
46 Gnawing animal like a rat (6)
48 Quarrel (4)

## No. 30

1 2 3 4 5 6 7 8
9 10 11
12
13 14 15
16 17 18 19
20 21 22 23 24 25 26
27
28 29 30
31 32
33 34 35
36
37 38 39
40 41 42 43 44 45 46
47 48 49
50
51 52 53

# No. 31

## Across

**9** Country in South West Asia (5,6)
**10** Well known for some bad deed (8)
**12** Group of six (9)
**13** Visually attractive (11)
**14** Infatuated (8)
**16** Food relish (5)
**19** Greenish-bronze fish (5)
**20** Official examination (10)
**22** Electrical component (9)
**25** Shuns (7)
**28** Milieu (11)
**30** Inattentive (11)
**31** Astonish (7)
**33** Operated by air under pressure (9)
**35** Usually (10)
**37** Benefactor (5)
**39** TV presenters (5)
**42** Training college for the priesthood (8)
**44** US hip-hop group whose hits include 'Intergalactic' (7,4)
**45** Waterproofed canvas (9)
**46** The West (8)
**47** Satisfactory (2,2,7)

## Down

**1** Gatherings of people (10)
**2** Allocations (6)
**3** Graceful (of movement) (8)
**4** Like many peanuts (6)
**5** Thin layer of sedimentary rock (6)
**6** Pertaining to life (6)
**7** Force that causes rotation (6)
**8** Greatly respect (6)
**11** Sour in taste (7)
**15** Weigh down (7)
**16** Sanctimonious (11)
**17** Revealed (9)
**18** Sells abroad (7)
**21** Examples (9)
**23** Recurrent topic (5)
**24** Hear a court case anew (5)
**25** Supply with; furnish (5)
**26** Near (5)
**27** Extend an arm or leg (7)
**29** Atomic particle (7)
**32** Ephemeral; unscrupulous (3-2-5)
**34** Deserved (7)
**36** Mathematical skill (8)
**37** Person who owes money (6)
**38** Subtle variation (6)
**40** Planetary paths around the sun (6)
**41** Lymphoid organ (6)
**42** Humorous television drama (6)
**43** Sharpness of vision (6)

*No. 31*

*No. 32*

## Across

1 Coldplay's second studio album (1,4,2,5,2,3,4)
12 Places (9)
13 Elucidates by using an example (11)
14 Conspicuous (7)
15 Corpulent (5)
16 Animal that eats bamboo (5)
17 Type of chemical bond (5)
19 Become more precipitous (7)
20 Donation (12)
22 Willing to do something (4)
24 Send someone to a medical specialist (5)
25 Action of ceasing to work (10)
28 Change gradually (6)
30 Bitterly pungent (5)
32 Strong drink (3)
33 Seize firmly (5)
35 Stationery item for removing mistakes (6)
37 Carelessness (10)
40 Up and about (5)
41 Hilltop (4)
43 Swimming technique (12)
46 Lessens (7)
48 Angry (5)
50 Balearic island (5)
51 Buffalo (5)
52 Helicopter (7)
53 Of a generous disposition (4-7)
54 Showing no enthusiasm (9)
55 Adventure novel by Alexandre Dumas (3,5,2,5,6)

## Down

1 Books of maps (7)
2 Not necessary (8,3)
3 Easily angered (3-8)
4 Moving on the surface of water (8)
5 Insole (anag.) (6)
6 River in South America (7)
7 Greatest in height (7)
8 Sense experience (5)
9 Delight beyond measure (9)
10 Wide-ranging (9)
11 Contempt (7)
18 Shipping hazards (8)
21 Figures of speech (6)
23 Tool for making holes in leather (3)
24 Large quantities of paper (5)
25 Recollect (8)
26 Make imperfect (3)
27 Come to a point (5)
29 States as one's opinion (6)
31 Sprite (3)
33 A parent's Mum (11)
34 Expects to happen (11)
36 Commotion (3)
38 Compliance (9)
39 Type of nut (9)
42 Remains of something damaged (8)
43 Cut of meat (7)
44 Italian dish (7)
45 Domain (7)
47 Hot wind blowing from North Africa (7)
49 Reach a specified level (6)
51 Organ situated in the skull (5)

## No. 32

1 2 3 4 5 6 7 8 9 10 11
12 13
14 15 16
17 18
19 20 21
22 23
24 25 26 27
28 29
30 31 32 33 34
35 36
37 38 39 40
41 42
43 44 45 46 47
48 49
50 51 52
53 54
55

*No. 33*

## Across

1 Knot with a double loop (3)
11 Japanese flower arranging (7)
12 Move unsteadily (6)
13 Word that identifies a thing (4)
14 Introverted (3)
15 Simon & Garfunkel song (3,5,2,7)
16 Took small bites out of (7)
18 Goal (3)
20 Passes into a solution (9)
22 Neck-warming garments (7)
24 Lesser (5)
25 European country (7)
26 Where you sleep (7)
27 Make room for (11)
33 Form into a cluster (11)
36 Movement of vehicles en masse (7)
38 Not outside (7)
40 Of sedate character (5)
41 Elevate (7)
42 Gauge (9)
44 Piece of wood (3)
46 Convey a thought in words (7)
48 Founder of the Scout Movement (6,5-6)
50 Add together (3)
51 Ring a bell (4)
52 Batting order (4-2)
53 Prompting device (7)
54 Domestic animal (3)

## Down

1 Tasteless showiness (9)
2 Lean and sinewy (4)
3 Pertaining to the teeth (6)
4 Children's toy (12)
5 Eastern temple (6)
6 Amaze (4)
7 Woodwind instrument (8)
8 Come up with ideas as a group (10)
9 Imaginary (6)
10 Restrained (11)
17 Large cushion for sitting on (7)
19 Ray (5)
21 Small truck (3)
23 Record on tape (5)
24 Venomous African snake (5)
28 Quoted (5)
29 Calculations of dimensions (12)
30 Proposal of marriage; bid (5)
31 Assign (7)
32 State of being well known (11)
34 Commercial (10)
35 Electronic message (5)
37 Person who expects the worst (9)
39 Performed an action (3)
40 Finely chopped (8)
43 Models of excellence (6)
45 Worldwide (6)
47 Contract of insurance (6)
49 Short sleeps (4)
50 Ooze (4)

# *No. 33*

1 2 3 4 5 6 7 8 9 10
11 12 13
14 15
16 17 18 19 20 21
22 23 24 25
26 27 28 29 30 31
32
33 34 35 36
37
38 39 40 41
42 43 44 45 46 47
48 49 50
51 52 53
54

*No. 34*

## Across

**1** Relating to the ear (9)
**6** Deserving affection (7)
**10** Fall behind (3)
**12** John Denver song originally known as 'Babe, I Hate to Go' (7,2,1,3,5)
**13** Heavy stick used as a weapon (4)
**14** Capital of Scotland (9)
**16** Sweet food courses (8)
**17** Greasy (4)
**18** Extremely impressive (11)
**21** Small stone (6)
**23** Current unit (3)
**25** Guarantees (7)
**27** Move out the way of (8)
**29** Absurd representation of something (8)
**30** Musical performance (7)
**31** Capital of Chile (8)
**33** Supported (8)
**35** Ancient parchment (7)
**38** Female sheep (3)
**39** Cease (6)
**40** Very successful (of a book) (4-7)
**42** Gemstone (4)
**44** Makes remote; cuts off (8)
**46** Of very high quality (3-6)
**48** Metallic element (4)
**49** Type of butterfly (5,13)
**51** Expected at a certain time (3)
**52** Most obese (7)
**53** Frequently (9)

## Down

**1** Get even for (6)
**2** Able to be turned round (10)
**3** Talk with (8)
**4** Female big cat (7)
**5** Preparedness (9)
**6** Made-up statement (3)
**7** Venomous snake (5)
**8** Overly self-assertive (5)
**9** Voters (10)
**11** Type of porridge (5)
**15** Tribe (anag.) (5)
**19** Large fortified buildings (7)
**20** Reptile (6)
**22** e.g. Abu Dhabi (7)
**24** Oceanic birds (7)
**25** With reference to (7)
**26** Oneness (5)
**28** Expresses gratitude (6)
**32** Musical symbol (6,4)
**34** Investigative job (10)
**36** Directly opposite in character (5)
**37** Fresh precipitation (9)
**39** Push button by a house (8)
**41** Encircling with a belt (7)
**43** Examined furtively (5)
**45** Give a job to (6)
**46** Fortune-telling card (5)
**47** Annoy (5)
**50** Widely cultivated cereal grass (3)

No. 34

*No. 35*

## Across

**9** Final (8)
**11** Unthinking (11)
**12** Room used by astronomers (11)
**13** Having a repeated design (9)
**14** Mediterranean island country (5)
**15** Snake toxin (5)
**18** Periods of very low rainfall (8)
**20** Fossil fuel (9)
**22** Occurring just before an event (4-6)
**24** Proficiently (11)
**26** Orange vegetables (7)
**29** Weighs down (7)
**31** Obstacle; barrier (11)
**32** Feeling annoyance (10)
**34** Being (9)
**36** Eternal (8)
**39** Way in (5)
**42** The beginning of an era (5)
**45** Scare mobs (anag.) (9)
**46** Instantly (11)
**47** Unambiguous (11)
**48** And so on (2,6)

## Down

**1** Implement change (6)
**2** Small carnivorous mammal (6)
**3** Happy; carefree (6)
**4** Dual audio (6)
**5** Leapt (6)
**6** Internet meeting place (4,4)
**7** Scarcity (6)
**8** Appraisal (10)
**10** Cyclone (7)
**15** TV audience (7)
**16** Worms used to control pests (9)
**17** Pamper (11)
**19** Non-specific (7)
**20** Eats like a bird (5)
**21** Shy (5)
**23** Growing old (9)
**25** Oval shape (7)
**26** Prove; attest (7)
**27** The Hunter (constellation) (5)
**28** Scorch (5)
**30** Hall or seating area (10)
**33** Relating to critical explanation (8)
**35** Adolescent (7)
**37** Garner; collect (6)
**38** Call for the presence of (6)
**40** Agile (6)
**41** Smelt strongly (6)
**43** Complied with a command (6)
**44** Period of prosperity (6)

*No. 35*

*No. 36*

**Across**

**10** French fashion designer (6)
**11** Using both letters and numbers (14)
**12** Desire to act (4)
**13** Deer-like ruminants (9)
**15** Not real or genuine (6)
**16** Slip up (3)
**17** e.g. March and May (6)
**19** Opposite of a winner (5)
**21** Unbending (10)
**22** Gasping for air (10)
**25** Small shelter (3)
**27** Female pronoun (3)
**29** Medley of dried petals (9)
**31** Animal fodder (3)
**32** Hard tooth coating (6)
**34** Distant (3)
**35** Belonging to an earlier time (6)
**36** e.g. almond or pecan (3)
**37** Senior manager (9)
**38** Pair of performers (3)
**39** Mineral spring (3)
**41** Remove salt from (10)
**43** Pertaining to language (10)
**46** Gemstones (5)
**48** Deep gorge (6)
**50** Foot extremity (3)
**51** Coiffure (6)
**53** Egg-laying mammal (9)
**55** Playthings (4)
**56** Groups of stars (14)
**57** SI unit of thermodynamic temperature (6)

**Down**

**1** Art of planning a dance (12)
**2** Arthropod (6)
**3** Earnest appeal (4)
**4** Fortress in Paris (8)
**5** Falls out unintentionally (6)
**6** Short story or poem for children (7,5)
**7** Daydream (7)
**8** Wist (anag.) (4)
**9** Animated drawings (8)
**14** South American country (4)
**18** Educated (8)
**20** Servile flattery (9)
**23** Collection of poems (9)
**24** Changes position (6)
**26** Thin strand of cotton (6)
**28** Form of government (8)
**30** Not special (3-2-3-4)
**33** Decomposition by a current (12)
**40** Aromatic spice (8)
**42** Anxious uncertainty (8)
**44** Chanted (7)
**45** Piece of metal used as money (4)
**47** Something done (6)
**49** Stinging weed (6)
**52** Relax and do little (4)
**54** Large deer (pl.) (4)

# *No. 36*

1 2 3 4 5 6 7 8 9
10 11
12 13 14 15
16
17 18 19 20
21
22 23 24
25 26 27 28
29 30 31 32 33
34
35 36 37
38 39
40 41 42
43 44 45
46 47 48 49
50
51 52 53 54 55
56 57

## No. 37

### Across

**1** Promotional book descriptions (6)
**4** Military observation of an area to gain information (14)
**10** Shout of appreciation (5)
**13** State of balance (11)
**15** Spiny egg-laying mammal (7)
**17** Left one's job (8)
**19** Kept hold of (8)
**20** Our planet (5)
**23** Money spent (11)
**25** Lunatic (6)
**26** Gull-like bird (4)
**28** Aromatic vegetable (5)
**29** Actress who played Rachel in 'Friends' (8,7)
**32** Bursts (4)
**34** Letters and parcels generally (4)
**36** Director of the film 'The Sixth Sense' (1,5,9)
**40** Brazilian dance (5)
**41** Freezes over (4)
**42** Most recent (6)
**43** Relation by marriage (6-2-3)
**46** Protective garment worn in the kitchen (5)
**48** Exclamations of protest (8)
**49** Simple and unsophisticated (8)
**51** West Indian musical style (7)
**53** Ordinary (11)
**55** Doctrine; system of beliefs (5)
**58** In a beneficial manner (14)
**59** Fit for consumption (6)

### Down

**1** Move up and down on water (3)
**2** North American nation (abbrev.) (3)
**3** Group of countries in an alliance (4)
**4** Evergreen shrub (12)
**5** Tidy (5,2)
**6** Words that identify things (5)
**7** Entirely (3)
**8** Stirred (anag.) (7)
**9** Fighting between armed forces (6)
**11** Defector (8)
**12** Annoyance (8)
**14** Action of setting something on fire (8)
**16** Shackle (8)
**18** Admit to a post (6)
**21** Greek writer of fables (5)
**22** Become husky (7)
**24** Illuminate (9)
**27** Small hill (5)
**29** Island in the West Indies (7)
**30** Sound of any kind (5)
**31** Dreamy; odd and unfamiliar (12)
**33** Work surface (8)
**35** Rope with a running noose (5)
**36** In a direct and frank way (3,2,3)
**37** Son of Daedalus in Greek mythology (6)
**38** Earlier in time (8)
**39** Responded to (8)
**44** Brutal; cruel (7)
**45** Surgical knives (7)
**47** Positioned (6)
**50** Musical instrument with keys (5)
**52** Move fast in a straight line (4)
**54** Breed of dog (3)
**56** Recede (3)
**57** Lyric poem (3)

*No. 37*

*No. 38*

## Across

**9** Feeling of hatred (11)
**10** Imaginary (8)
**12** Uncompromising demand (9)
**13** Potential (11)
**14** Without fortune (8)
**16** Pertaining to bees (5)
**19** Not clearly stated (5)
**20** Activity of writing articles (10)
**22** Letters are put in these (9)
**25** Stem the flow of (4,3)
**28** Speak in a slow manner (5)
**29** Sing softly (5)
**30** Indian monetary unit (5)
**31** Section of a long poem (5)
**32** Ring-shaped (7)
**34** Land nearly surrounded by water (9)
**36** Speech sounds that are not vowels (10)
**38** Misplaces (5)
**40** Vegetables (5)
**43** Chamber leading to a larger space (8)
**45** Pertaining to office workers (5-6)
**46** Large semiaquatic reptile (9)
**47** Stirring one's interest (8)
**48** Domineering (11)

## Down

**1** Shout of joy (10)
**2** Group of 12 constellations (6)
**3** Formal curse by a pope (8)
**4** What philatelists collect (6)
**5** Catch or snare (6)
**6** Spanish festival (6)
**7** Jumping into water (6)
**8** Erase (6)
**11** Rude (7)
**15** Form of singing for entertainment (7)
**16** The military (5,6)
**17** Repetition of a process (9)
**18** Short story (7)
**21** Suggest indirectly (9)
**23** Go about stealthily (5)
**24** Acoustic detection system (5)
**25** Parts (anag.) (5)
**26** Remove, as a badge (5)
**27** Pertaining to actuality (7)
**29** Mythical being (7)
**33** Gathering of people (10)
**35** Beginning to exist (7)
**37** Antique; obsolete (8)
**38** Restrained and subtle (3-3)
**39** Informer (6)
**41** Expression of praise (6)
**42** Horn (6)
**43** Agreement (6)
**44** Establish by law (6)

# *No. 38*

1 2 3 4 5 6 7 8
9 10 11
12 13
14 15 16 17 18 19
20 21 22 23 24
25 26 27 28 29
30 31 32 33
34 35 36 37
38 39 40 41 42 43 44
45 46
47 48

## No. 39

### Across

**1** For a very long time (5,3,4,4,4)
**10** Close-fitting hat (3)
**11** Network points where lines intersect (5)
**14** Next after sixth (7)
**15** Plans (7)
**16** Removes the lid (5)
**17** Epoch (3)
**18** Pellucid (5)
**21** Chemical element (3)
**22** Predatory fish (7)
**23** Easy to deal with (13)
**25** Trap; ensnare (3)
**27** Harmful (11)
**30** e.g. India and Spain (9)
**31** Rigid (5)
**33** Give tonic (anag.) (9)
**35** Consumer of food (5)
**36** Technical equipment (9)
**38** Plant-eating insect (11)
**42** Rodent (3)
**43** Informal expression (13)
**45** Newspaper audience (7)
**48** Beer (3)
**49** Snow and rain mix (5)
**52** Long period of time (3)
**53** Red cosmetic powder (5)
**55** Provoked; encouraged (7)
**56** Upstart; one who has recently gained wealth (7)
**57** Danger (5)
**58** Annoy (3)
**59** Animated film of 2010 featuring a Viking teenager named Hiccup (3,2,5,4,6)

### Down

**1** Unfasten (7)
**2** Very sensitive (of information) (3,6)
**3** Make less heavy (7)
**4** House of a recluse (9)
**5** Speech sound that is not a vowel (9)
**6** Pace (4)
**7** Make in bulk (4-7)
**8** Total disorder (5)
**9** Background actor (5)
**12** Style of Greek architecture (5)
**13** Of enormous effect (7)
**19** Snobbish (7)
**20** Record-keeping official (9)
**24** Decorative style of design (3,4)
**26** Knowledge (abbrev.) (4)
**27** Moves away from (9)
**28** Raging fire (7)
**29** Not telling the truth (5)
**32** Sudden inclination to act (7)
**33** e.g. a lemon or lime (6,5)
**34** Document allowing entry to a country (4)
**37** Shock physically (5-2)
**39** Nocturnal insect-eating mammal (9)
**40** Framework for moving the injured (9)
**41** Coming before (9)
**44** Opposite of outer (5)
**46** One more (7)
**47** Make less taut (7)
**50** Animal restraint (5)
**51** Act of stealing (5)
**54** ___ Halliwell: one of the Spice Girls (4)

*No. 39*

## No. 40

### Across

**9** Steep in (7)
**10** Papal court (5)
**11** One who makes beer (6)
**12** Pro (3)
**13** Form of oxygen found in the atmosphere (5)
**14** Remainder (7)
**15** Egg-shaped solids (6)
**16** Anticlimax (8)
**18** Able to use both hands well (12)
**20** Great energy (8)
**24** Daily periodicals (10)
**27** Receded (5)
**28** Clarets (4)
**30** Welsh emblem (4)
**31** Supervise (7)
**32** Shackle (7)
**33** Loose hood (4)
**34** Church service (4)
**36** Lazes; does nothing (5)
**37** Capital of Denmark (10)
**38** Exhibit; display (8)
**40** Absolute authority in any sphere (12)
**43** Loss of feeling (8)
**47** The Bull (star sign) (6)
**48** Just beginning to show promise (7)
**49** Belonging to them (5)
**50** Attempt to do (3)
**51** Emotionally dependent (6)
**52** Ring-shaped object (5)
**53** Giggles (7)

### Down

**1** Japanese dress (6)
**2** Enforce compliance with (6)
**3** European country (6)
**4** Kept private; unknown by others (6)
**5** High-capacity internet access (9)
**6** Dagger handle (4)
**7** Biography from personal knowledge (6)
**8** Main premises of a company (12)
**10** Similar (10)
**11** Borough of New York City (5)
**16** Lowest point (5)
**17** Vitality (3)
**19** Drabness (9)
**21** Forgive (7)
**22** Bring an accusation against (7)
**23** Person who delivers news (9)
**25** Inactive pill (7)
**26** Strong verbal attack (7)
**29** Thriftily (12)
**32** Increases greatly in number (10)
**35** Garden buildings (5)
**36** Not in possession of the facts (2,3,4)
**39** What a spider weaves (3)
**41** Growing weary (6)
**42** Petulant (5)
**43** Invalidate; nullify (6)
**44** Short choral compositions (6)
**45** Required (6)
**46** State of mental strain (6)
**48** Computer memory unit (4)

## No. 40

1 2 3 4 5 6 7 8
9 10 11
12
13 14 15
16 17 18 19
20 21 22 23 24 25 26
27
28 29 30
31 32
33 34 35
36
37 38 39
40 41 42 43 44 45 46
47 48 49
50
51 52 53

## No. 41

### Across

**1** Time that is to come (6)
**4** Belief in one's own ability (4-10)
**10** Implant (5)
**13** Tendency to disintegrate (11)
**15** Captain's record (7)
**17** Defeated (8)
**19** Cocktail (8)
**20** Period between childhood and adulthood (5)
**23** Person with strong patriotic feelings (11)
**25** Contemporary (6)
**26** Pairs (4)
**28** Tall structure on a castle (5)
**29** Individuality (15)
**32** Religious act (4)
**34** Anti-aircraft fire (4)
**36** Dependability (15)
**40** Third Greek letter (5)
**41** US actress and singer (4)
**42** Recompense for hardship (6)
**43** Increasing greatly in number (11)
**46** Body of water (5)
**48** Board used to display adverts (8)
**49** Ornamental climbing plant (8)
**51** Figurative language (7)
**53** Illogical (11)
**55** Organic compound (5)
**58** Occasionally; periodically (14)
**59** Took part in a game (6)

### Down

**1** Enemy (3)
**2** Bath vessel (3)
**3** Repeat (4)
**4** Small meteor (8,4)
**5** Exclusion from the workplace (7)
**6** Waterslide (5)
**7** Pen point (3)
**8** Domestic beasts of burden (7)
**9** Small box (6)
**11** Type of pasta (8)
**12** Fluent in the use of language (8)
**14** Pamphlets (8)
**16** Smiling broadly (8)
**18** Fester (6)
**21** Semiaquatic mammal (5)
**22** Hurries (7)
**24** List of wares (9)
**27** Produce a literary work (5)
**29** Actually; in reality (2,5)
**30** Raised floor or platform (5)
**31** Immediately (12)
**33** Paucity (8)
**35** Destiny; fate (5)
**36** Sharpness (of taste) (8)
**37** Ideally perfect state (6)
**38** In these times (8)
**39** Love song (8)
**44** Uncertain (7)
**45** Clear perception (7)
**47** Vertical pillar (6)
**50** Garbage or drivel (5)
**52** Case of film (4)
**54** Make a choice (3)
**56** Your (poetic) (3)
**57** Fishing pole (3)

# *No. 41*

1 2 3 4 5 6 7 8 9
10 11 12 13 14
15 16
17 18
19 20 21 22
23 24
25 26 27
28
29 30 31 32
33
34 35 36 37 38 39
40
41 42
43 44 45
46 47 48
49 50
51 52
53 54 55 56 57
58 59

*No. 42*

## Across

**9** Angry dispute (11)
**10** Vision (8)
**12** Similarities (9)
**13** Disenchant (11)
**14** Surpass in excellence (8)
**16** Tiny (5)
**19** Large bird of prey (5)
**20** Island in the Indian Ocean (10)
**22** Type of restaurant (9)
**25** Mournful (7)
**28** Spoken communication (4,2,5)
**30** One in charge of a school (4,7)
**31** At a greater distance (7)
**33** Gradual increase in loudness (9)
**35** Aired (10)
**37** Large spoon with a long handle (5)
**39** Coming after (5)
**42** More attractive (8)
**44** Enthusiastic supporter (11)
**45** Thankfulness (9)
**46** Ant email (anag.) (8)
**47** Relating to fireworks (11)

## Down

**1** Beyond the scope of scientific understanding (10)
**2** Narrow passage of water (6)
**3** Representations or descriptions of data (8)
**4** Stagnation or inactivity (6)
**5** Weak through age or illness (6)
**6** Servile (6)
**7** Getting older (6)
**8** Attitude or body position (6)
**11** Learner (7)
**15** War carriage (7)
**16** Tool; cocktail (11)
**17** Find out (9)
**18** Rise into the air (of an aircraft) (4,3)
**21** Fierce and intense (of a situation) (3-6)
**23** Rocky; harsh (5)
**24** Loathe (5)
**25** Principle of morality (5)
**26** Rub out (5)
**27** Choice for a television viewer (7)
**29** Biting (7)
**32** Final result (3,7)
**34** V-shaped mark (7)
**36** Utters repeatedly (8)
**37** Residents of an area (6)
**38** Imagined whilst asleep (6)
**40** Astonished (6)
**41** Free from a liability (6)
**42** Common bird (6)
**43** Purpose (6)

*No. 42*

1 2 3 4 5 6 7 8
9 10 11
12 13
14 15 16 17 18 19
20 21 22 23 24
25 26 27 28 29
30 31 32
33 34 35 36
37 38 39 40 41 42 43
44 45
46 47

## No. 43

### Across

**1** Mark Twain novel (3,6,3,3,6)
**12** Robber (9)
**13** Capital of Argentina (6,5)
**14** Volcanic crater (7)
**15** Money (5)
**16** Cancel (5)
**17** Machine for shaping wood or metal (5)
**19** Tallier (anag.) (7)
**20** Regardless of (12)
**22** Three feet length (4)
**24** Wading bird (5)
**25** Successful book (10)
**28** Taxonomic groupings (6)
**30** Clearance events (5)
**32** Court (3)
**33** Fills a suitcase (5)
**35** Public speaker (6)
**37** Particularly (10)
**40** Should (5)
**41** Mischievous god in Norse mythology (4)
**43** Clearness (12)
**46** Insensitive and cruel (7)
**48** Foot joint (5)
**50** Extreme (5)
**51** Ball of lead (5)
**52** Amusing (7)
**53** Apotheosis (11)
**54** Financial inducement (9)
**55** US rock band whose vocalist is Zack de la Rocha (4,7,3,7)

### Down

**1** Average (7)
**2** Type of triangle (11)
**3** Misleading clues (3,8)
**4** Usually (8)
**5** Straying from the right course (6)
**6** One who eats a bit at a time (7)
**7** Molasses (7)
**8** Decay (5)
**9** Large mass of sliding snow (9)
**10** Enduring (9)
**11** Decide firmly (7)
**18** Refuge (8)
**21** Document granting invention rights (6)
**23** Playing card (3)
**24** Speed (5)
**25** Borough of New York City (8)
**26** Grassland (3)
**27** Restore factory settings (5)
**29** US state whose capital is Carson City (6)
**31** Make a living with difficulty (3)
**33** Posing a difficulty (11)
**34** Experts on a subject (11)
**36** Ancient boat (3)
**38** Toy (9)
**39** Country in Central America (5,4)
**42** Frozen dessert (3,5)
**43** Loud sound following lightning (7)
**44** Act of avoiding capture (7)
**45** Piece of furniture (7)
**47** Spend lavishly (7)
**49** Brandy distilled from cherries (6)
**51** Public square (5)

*No. 43*

1 2 3 4 5 6 7 8 9 10 11
12 13
14 15 16
17 18
19 20 21
22 23
24 25 26 27
28 29
30 31 32 33 34
35 36
37 38 39 40
41 42
43 44 45 46 47
48 49
50 51 52
53 54
55

*No. 44*

## Across

**10** Continent (6)
**11** Police rank (14)
**12** Cried (4)
**13** Window dummy (9)
**15** Confine as a prisoner (6)
**16** Turn upside down (3)
**17** Infinitesimally small (6)
**19** Hushed (5)
**21** Absolute (10)
**22** Squeezed (10)
**25** Curved shape (3)
**27** Secret agent (3)
**29** Logarithm (anag.) (9)
**31** Smack (3)
**32** Whole (6)
**34** Snow runner (3)
**35** Recover (6)
**36** Sticky substance (3)
**37** Intermediary (9)
**38** Command to a horse (3)
**39** Born (3)
**41** Not moving (10)
**43** Exhaustively (10)
**46** Unabridged (5)
**48** Protects (6)
**50** Polite address for a man (3)
**51** Art of growing dwarfed trees (6)
**53** Thing with no special qualities (9)
**55** Imperial unit (4)
**56** Foolish search for something unattainable (4,5,5)
**57** Lived by (6)

## Down

**1** Loving (12)
**2** Person subject to an attack (6)
**3** Heat up (4)
**4** Giant ocean waves (8)
**5** Positive and happy (6)
**6** Indifferent to (12)
**7** Instructions on how to cook dishes (7)
**8** Modify (4)
**9** Etched into a surface (8)
**14** Official language of Pakistan (4)
**18** Urging on (8)
**20** Artisan (9)
**23** Elaborate display (9)
**24** Small oval plum (6)
**26** Makes a ringing sound (6)
**28** Compliant; submissive (8)
**30** Fellowship (12)
**33** Showed not to be true (12)
**40** Grandiosity of language (8)
**42** Achieved (8)
**44** 20th letter of the Greek alphabet (7)
**45** Chinese monetary unit (4)
**47** Strong cloth used to make sails (6)
**49** ___ Keys: US singer (6)
**52** Team (4)
**54** 365 days (4)

## *No. 44*

1 2 3 4 5 6 7 8 9
10 11
12 13 14 15
16
17 18 19 20
21
22 23 24
25 26 27 28
29 30 31 32 33
34
35 36 37
38 39
40 41 42
43 44 45
46 47 48 49
50
51 52 53 54 55
56 57

*No. 45*

## Across

**1** Fastening devices (6)
**4** Type of meeting for people in different locations (14)
**10** Consecrate (5)
**13** Devices popular before computers existed (11)
**15** Seed with a fibrous husk and edible white flesh (7)
**17** Form the base for (8)
**19** Stalemate (5-3)
**20** Anxiety (5)
**23** Form of energy (11)
**25** Minds (6)
**26** Roman god of war (4)
**28** Journeys (5)
**29** Famous monument in Berlin (11,4)
**32** Small mountain (4)
**34** Blunder (4)
**36** Calmness when under pressure or emotional (15)
**40** Flowering plant (5)
**41** Right to hold property (4)
**42** On a ship or train (6)
**43** Act of staying away from work (11)
**46** Unfortunately (5)
**48** Idleness (8)
**49** Corrosive precipitation (4,4)
**51** In the place of (7)
**53** Weak form of illumination (11)
**55** Sells (5)
**58** Canadian singer known for the song 'Call Me Maybe' (5,3,6)
**59** Number of Apostles (6)

## Down

**1** Round loaf of bread (3)
**2** Consumed food (3)
**3** Monetary unit of Mexico (4)
**4** Capable of being moved (12)
**5** Salad vegetable (7)
**6** Managed to deal with (5)
**7** Of recent origin (3)
**8** Backtrack (7)
**9** Universe (6)
**11** University teacher (8)
**12** Metrical analysis of verse (8)
**14** Move (8)
**16** Covered walk in a convent (8)
**18** Archimedes' famous cry (6)
**21** Insect larva (5)
**22** Scuffles (7)
**24** Congeal (9)
**27** Apart from (5)
**29** Baffles (7)
**30** Opposite of below (5)
**31** Act of sending a message (12)
**33** Discrete; distinct (8)
**35** Ultimate (5)
**36** Elks idea (anag.) (8)
**37** Winner (6)
**38** Midday (8)
**39** Encircle (8)
**44** Eventually (2,3,2)
**45** Sets fire to (7)
**47** Spiny tree or shrub (6)
**50** Debate in a heated manner (5)
**52** Affirm solemnly (4)
**54** Sheltered side (3)
**56** Zero (3)
**57** Female pronoun (3)

No. 45

1 2 3 4 5 6 7 8 9
10 11 12 13 14
15 16
17 18
19 20 21 22
23 24
25 26 27
28
29 30 31 32
33
34 35 36 37 38 39
40
41 42
43 44 45
46 47 48
49 50
51 52
53 54 55 56 57
58 59

## *No. 46*

### Across

**9** Connoisseur (7)
**10** Musical note (5)
**11** Multiples of twenty (6)
**12** Beam of light (3)
**13** Gold block (5)
**14** Tall stand used by a preacher (7)
**15** Mocked (6)
**16** Occurring regularly (8)
**18** Contentment (12)
**20** Mental considerations (8)
**24** Final demands (10)
**27** Coral reef (5)
**28** Locate or place (4)
**30** Skin condition on the face (4)
**31** Shorten (7)
**32** Public transport vehicle (7)
**33** Heavenly body (4)
**34** Throw a coin in the air (4)
**36** Brown nut (5)
**37** Very typical of a kind of person (10)
**38** Cherish; preserve (8)
**40** Hostile aggressiveness (12)
**43** Very plentiful (8)
**47** Yellowish-brown pigment (6)
**48** Prevented (7)
**49** Paved area (5)
**50** Hairpiece (3)
**51** Welcomes (6)
**52** Customary (5)
**53** Decorative framework (7)

### Down

**1** Aloof (6)
**2** Chess piece (6)
**3** Single-celled alga (6)
**4** Play boisterously (6)
**5** Indignant (9)
**6** Plant with fronds (4)
**7** Burrowing marsupial (6)
**8** Changes to a situation (12)
**10** Swimming stroke (10)
**11** Country in the Middle East (5)
**16** Assesses performance (5)
**17** Cuddle (3)
**19** Gloomy (9)
**21** Dig out of the ground (7)
**22** Coiffure (7)
**23** Abrasive used for smoothing (9)
**25** People who are in a club (7)
**26** Kitchen appliance (7)
**29** Middleman (12)
**32** Western (10)
**35** Perfume (5)
**36** Ample (9)
**39** Female chicken (3)
**41** Yearned for (6)
**42** Bites at persistently (5)
**43** Advance evidence for (6)
**44** Tennis official (6)
**45** Keep hold of (6)
**46** Loops with running knots (6)
**48** Fit of shivering (4)

# No. 46

1 2 3 4 5 6 7 8
9 10 11
12
13 14 15
16 17 18 19
20 21 22 23 24 25 26
27
28 29 30
31 32
33 34 35
36
37 38 39
40 41 42 43 44 45 46
47 48 49
50
51 52 53

*No. 47*

## Across

**9** Snowstorm (8)
**11** Fabricate (11)
**12** Overly polite (11)
**13** Gun dog (9)
**14** Bout of extravagant shopping (5)
**15** Trembling poplar (5)
**18** Woodwind instrument (8)
**20** Provide with fresh air (9)
**22** Insignificant (10)
**24** Tame (11)
**26** What a bodybuilder lifts (7)
**29** Confusing (7)
**31** Sparkle (11)
**32** Ahead of the times (10)
**34** Based on casual observations (of an account) (9)
**36** The whole of something (8)
**39** Water lily (5)
**42** Locates or places (5)
**45** Based on facts; plausible (9)
**46** Giant aerial (anag.) (11)
**47** Suggested or implied idea (11)
**48** Having no weak points (8)

## Down

**1** Calculating machine (6)
**2** Correspond to (6)
**3** Small whirlpools (6)
**4** Attribute to (6)
**5** Set of instructions (6)
**6** Highly seasoned smoked beef (8)
**7** Deep serving dish (6)
**8** Pique (10)
**10** River in Africa (7)
**15** Incredible (7)
**16** Widespread (9)
**17** Meaningless (11)
**19** Existing at the beginning (7)
**20** Russian spirit (5)
**21** Wanderer (5)
**23** Gad (9)
**25** Nerve impulses (7)
**26** Foolish (7)
**27** Vital part or essence (5)
**28** One of the senses (5)
**30** Dissimilarity (10)
**33** Individuality (8)
**35** Melody; a song (7)
**37** Covering a roof with thin slabs (6)
**38** Sailing vessels (6)
**40** Church instruments (6)
**41** Remove goods from a van (6)
**43** Unspecified objects (6)
**44** Deliberative assembly (6)

*No. 47*

*No. 48*

## Across

**9** Benefactors (6)
**11** Possessor (5)
**13** Connoisseur; gourmet (7)
**14** Cup (3)
**15** Discussion (6)
**16** Isolate (7)
**17** Verse form (5)
**18** Tamed (12)
**20** White flakes in the hair (8)
**23** Protest against official policy (10)
**26** Sending by sea (8)
**29** Waggish (5)
**30** Set in layers (6)
**31** Peas (anag.) (4)
**33** Male relation (5)
**35** Label (3)
**36** Frozen precipitation (4)
**37** Title placed before a name (6)
**38** Not concealed (5)
**40** Campaigner (8)
**42** Shaking of the ground (10)
**43** Shimmered (8)
**48** Exceptional (12)
**51** Exploiting unfairly (5)
**52** Starting points (7)
**54** Except when (6)
**55** Group of whales (3)
**56** Respectable; refined (7)
**57** Loosely-woven cloth (5)
**58** Make beloved (6)

## Down

**1** Best starting placement in a motor race (4,8)
**2** Find (6)
**3** Canines (4)
**4** Unharmed (9)
**5** Be contingent upon (6)
**6** Inside of (6)
**7** Lower in rank (6)
**8** Turn down (6)
**10** Refine metal (5)
**12** Type of road junction (10)
**19** Leader of the orchestra (9)
**21** Depression (3)
**22** Contrapuntal composition (5)
**24** Spreads out (7)
**25** Worked out logically (7)
**26** Idle people (9)
**27** Thoroughly (2,5)
**28** Flat highland (7)
**32** Spotless (5-3-4)
**34** All that exists (10)
**36** These keep your feet warm (5)
**39** Persistent and dogged (9)
**41** Put a question to (3)
**44** Fall quickly (6)
**45** Periods of rule (6)
**46** Carried with difficulty (6)
**47** Dribbles (6)
**49** Escape from (5)
**50** Deceive (6)
**53** Moved quickly (4)

## No. 48

1 2 3 4 5 6 7 8
9 10 11 12 13
14
15 16 17
18 19 20 21 22
23 24 25 26 27 28
29
30 31 32
33 34 35
36 37
38 39
40 41 42
43 44 45 46 47 48 49 50
51 52 53 54
55
56 57 58

*No. 49*

## Across

**1** Chatter (3)
**11** Novice driver (7)
**12** Tropical fruit (6)
**13** Liquid precipitation (4)
**14** Ground condensation (3)
**15** Having the opposite of the intended effect (17)
**16** Surround entirely (7)
**18** What a hen lays (3)
**20** Yellow flower (9)
**22** Type of respiration (7)
**24** Two times (5)
**25** Ditherer (7)
**26** Tapering stone pillar (7)
**27** Astound (11)
**33** Having high status (11)
**36** Equilateral parallelogram (7)
**38** Intrusions (7)
**40** Folded back part of a coat (5)
**41** Ardent (7)
**42** Assembly (9)
**44** Uncooked (of meat) (3)
**46** Table servers (7)
**48** Ballet written by Jean-Louis Vaudoyer (2,7,2,2,4)
**50** Lipid (3)
**51** Unit of land area (4)
**52** Bean (6)
**53** Perfect example of a quality (7)
**54** Use (anag.) (3)

## Down

**1** Award for first place (4,5)
**2** Exhaled hard (4)
**3** Package (6)
**4** Completely unaware of (12)
**5** Contort (6)
**6** Goad on (4)
**7** Capable of being used (8)
**8** Railing (10)
**9** Cheese shredder (6)
**10** Immoderate (11)
**17** Wordy (7)
**19** Great sorrow (5)
**21** Road vehicle (3)
**23** Sheep sound (5)
**24** Capital of Japan (5)
**28** Pertaining to the ear (5)
**29** Style of piano-based blues (6-6)
**30** Machine; automaton (5)
**31** Failure to be present (7)
**32** Thoroughly tidy the house (6,5)
**34** Incidentally (10)
**35** Wonderful (5)
**37** Easily offended (9)
**39** Degenerate (3)
**40** Woody (8)
**43** Jumped on one leg (6)
**45** Moves repeatedly from side to side (6)
**47** Refrigerator compartment (6)
**49** Pitcher (4)
**50** Enemies (4)

# *No. 49*

1 2 3 4 5 6 7 8 9 10
11 12 13
14 15
16 17 18 19 20 21
22 23 24 25
26 27 28 29 30 31
32
33 34 35 36
37
38 39 40 41
42 43 44 45 46 47
48 49 50
51 52 53
54

## *No. 50*

### Across

**9** e.g. anger or love (7)
**10** Means of mass communication (5)
**11** Slender (6)
**12** Secret retreat (3)
**13** Survived (5)
**14** A particular item (7)
**15** Surpass (6)
**16** Unthinking (of a response) (4-4)
**18** Extremely harmful (12)
**20** Bothers (8)
**24** Burdensome (10)
**27** Plant spike (5)
**28** Fine soft thread (4)
**30** Aerial tennis shots (4)
**31** Symbolic objects (7)
**32** European river (7)
**33** Basic unit of matter (4)
**34** Require (4)
**36** Longed for (5)
**37** Violate (10)
**38** Critical explanation (8)
**40** Having an efficient approach to one's work (12)
**43** Regularity of nature (8)
**47** Flash intermittently (6)
**48** Thus; as a result (7)
**49** Competes in a speed contest (5)
**50** Bashful; reluctant to give details (3)
**51** East (6)
**52** Tailored fold (5)
**53** One event in a sequence (7)

### Down

**1** Capital of Germany (6)
**2** Famous French museum (6)
**3** Poser; enigma (6)
**4** Uncover (6)
**5** Process of learning (9)
**6** Walk through water (4)
**7** Involuntary spasm (6)
**8** Hard to fathom (12)
**10** Precise; scrupulous (10)
**11** Derisive smile (5)
**16** Toys flown in the wind (5)
**17** Triangular sail (3)
**19** Supplant (9)
**21** Not tidy (7)
**22** Brazilian dance (7)
**23** Measure of gradient (9)
**25** Burst violently (7)
**26** Absence of sound (7)
**29** Preliminary (12)
**32** Process of dealing with people (10)
**35** Covered with powdery dirt (5)
**36** Outer boundary (9)
**39** Jewel (3)
**41** Removed creases from clothes (6)
**42** Upright (5)
**43** Fashions (6)
**44** Ghoulish; unhealthy (6)
**45** Cowers (anag.) (6)
**46** Hurried (6)
**48** Sort; variety (4)

# No. 50

## No. 51

### Across

**9** Unimaginable (11)
**10** Surpass (8)
**12** Outstandingly bad (9)
**13** Book lover (11)
**14** Blushing with embarrassment (3-5)
**16** Makes musical sounds (5)
**19** Targeted (5)
**20** Diplomatic official (10)
**22** Diving seabird (9)
**25** Layer or band of rock (7)
**28** Sustenance (11)
**30** Joint business (11)
**31** Holy place (7)
**33** Overwhelming majority of votes for one party (9)
**35** Unlucky (3-7)
**37** The reproduction of sound (5)
**39** One image within another (5)
**42** Short account of an incident (8)
**44** Supreme authority (11)
**45** Exercise of absolute power (9)
**46** Bushy-tailed rodent (8)
**47** Joyful occasion (11)

### Down

**1** Large and heavy vehicle (10)
**2** Be present at (6)
**3** Financial statements (8)
**4** Brought about (6)
**5** Third sign of the zodiac (6)
**6** Sharp bend in a road (3-3)
**7** Hackneyed statement (6)
**8** Attach (6)
**11** Highest singing voice (7)
**15** Squash (7)
**16** Fortified defensive position (11)
**17** Active at night (9)
**18** Short trips (7)
**21** Female offspring (9)
**23** Wide-awake (5)
**24** ___ pole: tribal emblem (5)
**25** Flower part; pales (anag.) (5)
**26** Broadcast again (5)
**27** Type of cocktail (7)
**29** Number of years in a century (7)
**32** Removing clothes (10)
**34** Cleaning item (7)
**36** Value greatly (8)
**37** Birthplace of St Francis (6)
**38** Pious (6)
**40** Small worry; irritate (6)
**41** Tempt (6)
**42** Mixed up or confused (6)
**43** Set of clothes (6)

*No. 51*

1 2 3 4 5 6 7 8
9 10 11
12 13
14 15 16 17 18 19
20 21 22 23 24
25 26 27 28 29
30 31 32
33 34 35 36
37 38 39 40 41 42 43
44 45
46 47

# No. 52

## Across

1 Gang (3)
11 Ignorant of something (7)
12 Willow twigs (6)
13 Possess (4)
14 Broad inlet of the sea (3)
15 Proverb suggesting one should not act without first considering the consequences (4,6,3,4)
16 Release (7)
18 Athletic facility (3)
20 First version of a device (9)
22 African country with capital Windhoek (7)
24 Killer whales (5)
25 e.g. shrimp or crab (7)
26 Belief (7)
27 Testimony (11)
33 Award for third place (6,5)
36 Military gestures (7)
38 Refutes; sends back (7)
40 Animal enclosures (5)
41 Opposite of later (7)
42 Edible plant (9)
44 Popular edible fish (3)
46 Fell quickly (7)
48 Just before it is too late (2,3,8,4)
50 Make less bright (3)
51 Wicked (4)
52 Seventh planet (6)
53 Country whose capital is Dublin (7)
54 Tree of the genus Quercus (3)

## Down

1 City in Australia (9)
2 Anchored float (4)
3 Spanish rice dish (6)
4 Provincialism (12)
5 Bloodsucking insect (6)
6 Bark of a dog (4)
7 Brings disorder to (8)
8 Variety; mixture (10)
9 Wooden house (6)
10 Radiant; sumptuous (11)
17 River of South East Africa (7)
19 Type of coffee drink (5)
21 Pay (anag.) (3)
23 Vigorous attack (5)
24 Possessed (5)
28 Long pointed elephant teeth (5)
29 Working for oneself (4-8)
30 Daisy-like flower (5)
31 Distributing (7)
32 Shortened (11)
34 Of external origin (10)
35 Good sense; reasoning (5)
37 Distinctive characteristic (9)
39 Run steadily (3)
40 Splitting (8)
43 Breathe out (6)
45 Garden flowering plant (6)
47 Raise up (6)
49 Overly curious (4)
50 Extinct bird (4)

*No. 52*

1 2 3 4 5 6 7 8 9 10
11 12 13
14 15
16 17 18 19 20 21
22 23 24 25
26 27 28 29 30 31
32
33 34 35 36
37
38 39 40 41
42 43 44 45 46 47
48 49 50
51 52 53
54

## No. 53

### Across

**9** Pursuit of high principles (8)
**11** Incorporating sound and images (11)
**12** Residents (11)
**13** Caustic (9)
**14** Employer (5)
**15** Make thirsty (5)
**18** Device that sends a rocket into space (8)
**20** Given to using irony (9)
**22** Presence at an event (10)
**24** Basically (11)
**26** Get rid of (4,3)
**29** Prayers (anag.) (7)
**31** Bitter; angry (of speech) (11)
**32** Related; connected (10)
**34** Bulbous plant (9)
**36** Enter unlawfully (8)
**39** Sediment (5)
**42** Tied, as shoes (5)
**45** Musical instrument (9)
**46** Youth (11)
**47** Masterpiece (4,2,5)
**48** Recondite (8)

### Down

**1** End (6)
**2** Current of air (6)
**3** Leaping antelope (6)
**4** Adhesive putty (6)
**5** Relating to government revenue (6)
**6** Capsize (8)
**7** Violent uprising (6)
**8** Clever foal (anag.) (10)
**10** Country in West Africa (7)
**15** Scare rigid (7)
**16** Remember (9)
**17** Unnecessarily forceful (5-6)
**19** Make rougher (7)
**20** Guide a vehicle (5)
**21** Exposes to danger (5)
**23** Permissible degree of variation (9)
**25** Becomes less wide (7)
**26** Photographic devices (7)
**27** Woodwind instruments (5)
**28** Clenched hands (5)
**30** Flexibility (10)
**33** Formed a mental concept of (8)
**35** Unlawful (7)
**37** Book of the Bible (6)
**38** Higher in rank (6)
**40** Like corduroy (6)
**41** Ship's kitchen (6)
**43** Unfounded story (6)
**44** Soak (6)

## No. 53

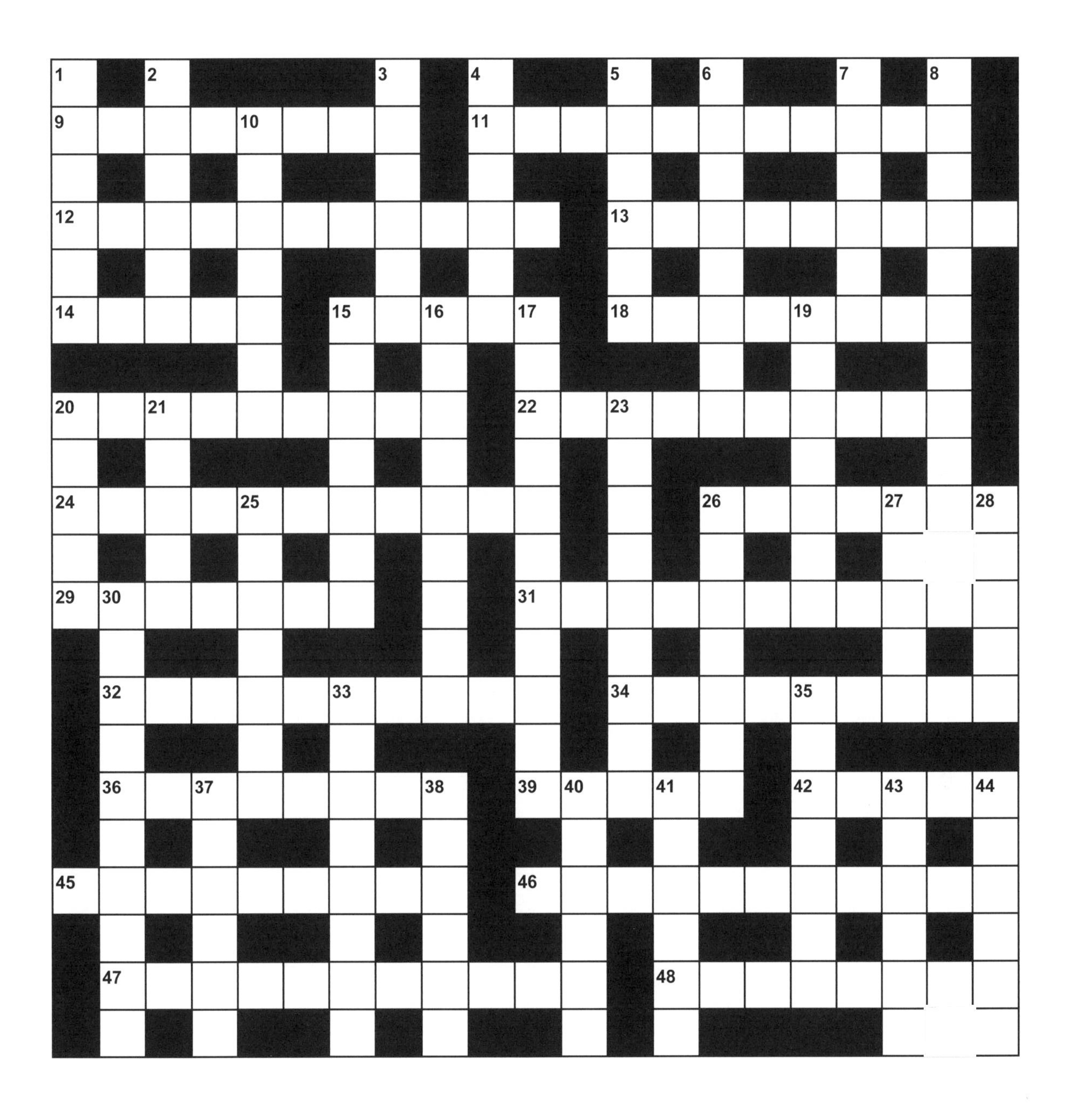

## No. 54

### Across

**9** Knocks down an opponent (6)
**11** Spread by scattering (5)
**13** Wavering effect in a musical tone (7)
**14** Frying pan (3)
**15** Electric generator (6)
**16** e.g. using a straw (7)
**17** Ancient object (5)
**18** Very sad (12)
**20** Where photographs are developed (8)
**23** Considerate (10)
**26** Sport (8)
**29** Microscopic fungus (5)
**30** Long and very narrow (6)
**31** Every (4)
**33** Challenged (5)
**35** Soft animal hair (3)
**36** Snares; bags (4)
**37** Boredom (6)
**38** Original (5)
**40** Large amphibian (8)
**42** Imprecise; wrong (10)
**43** Speed up (8)
**48** Ancient and old-fashioned (12)
**51** Rustic (5)
**52** Pretended (7)
**54** Heat; affection (6)
**55** Bristle-like appendage (3)
**56** Type of alcohol (7)
**57** Conventions (5)
**58** Having only magnitude (6)

### Down

**1** Do something high risk (4,4,4)
**2** Picture produced from many small pieces (6)
**3** Requests (4)
**4** Vitally (9)
**5** Put on a production (6)
**6** One who carries something (6)
**7** US monetary unit (6)
**8** Mexican cloak (6)
**10** Faint (5)
**12** Very dense star (5,5)
**19** Progeny (9)
**21** Clothing needed for an activity (3)
**22** Mixture that insulates soil (5)
**24** Object used in the kitchen (7)
**25** Jumping athlete (7)
**26** Right side of a boat (9)
**27** Frenzied (7)
**28** Electric appliance (7)
**32** Military judicial body (5,7)
**34** Practice of predicting the future (10)
**36** Admirable (5)
**39** People who tune into a radio show (9)
**41** Gave a meal to (3)
**44** Ancient Persian king (6)
**45** Hearts (anag.) (6)
**46** Doing nothing (6)
**47** Envelop (6)
**49** Areas of mown grass (5)
**50** Occurring in spring (6)
**53** Morse code symbol (4)

# No. 54

1 2 3 4 5 6 7 8
9 10 11 12 13
14
15 16 17
18 19 20 21 22
23 24 25 26 27 28
29
30 31 32
33 34 35
36 37
38 39
40 41 42
43 44 45 46 47 48 49 50
51 52 53 54
55
56 57 58

## No. 55

### Across

**1** Flatterer (9)
**6** Laugh unrestrainedly (5,2)
**10** Flee (3)
**12** Vegetable (9,9)
**13** Charges (4)
**14** Actors (9)
**16** Squid (8)
**17** Light beams (4)
**18** Express sympathy (11)
**21** Shining (6)
**23** Short sleep (3)
**25** Irritated (7)
**27** Move to another place (8)
**29** Component parts (8)
**30** Talk foolishly (7)
**31** State of the USA (8)
**33** Recently (8)
**35** Nervous (7)
**38** Fruit of a rose (3)
**39** Wild dog (6)
**40** Performer (11)
**42** Skin mark from a wound (4)
**44** Hostilities (8)
**46** Education (9)
**48** Popular martial art (4)
**49** Irish poet whose works include 'The Second Coming' (7,6,5)
**51** Insect which collects pollen (3)
**52** Highest vantage point of a building (7)
**53** Seriously (9)

### Down

**1** Afternoon snooze in Spain (6)
**2** Arthropod; e.g. crab or lobster (10)
**3** Apparition (8)
**4** Sterile (7)
**5** Workman; shopkeeper (9)
**6** Feline animal (3)
**7** Capital of Ghana (5)
**8** Speed in nautical miles per hour (5)
**9** Partiality (10)
**11** Destitute (5)
**15** Concealed; secret (5)
**19** Old (7)
**20** Fervent (6)
**22** Decorate food (7)
**24** Kneecap (7)
**25** One who settles a dispute (7)
**26** Fly around a planet (5)
**28** Struggled against (6)
**32** A very influential country (10)
**34** Feeling of eagerness and anticipation (10)
**36** Boise's state (5)
**37** Set up for a purpose (9)
**39** Large celebration (8)
**41** Frequent customer (7)
**43** Tiny piece of food (5)
**45** Hearty (anag.) (6)
**46** Group of shots (5)
**47** Robbery (5)
**50** Soak up; wipe away (3)

# No. 55

1 2 3 4 5 6 7 8 9
10 11
12
13
14 15
16 17
18 19 20
21 22 23 24
25 26
27 28 29
30
31 32 33 34
35 36 37
38 39
40 41
42 43 44 45
46 47
48
49 50
51
52 53

*No. 56*

## Across

**9** Workshop or studio (7)
**10** Pretend (5)
**11** Resembling a horse (6)
**12** Annoy (3)
**13** Entertain (5)
**14** Smooth and soft (7)
**15** Saturated (6)
**16** SE Asian country (8)
**18** Completeness (12)
**20** Access code (8)
**24** Competition (10)
**27** Thermosetting resin (5)
**28** Plant stalk (4)
**30** Pen points (4)
**31** Financial gains (7)
**32** Moved slowly (7)
**33** Small flake of soot (4)
**34** Grain (4)
**36** Committee (5)
**37** Tolerant; non-restrictive (10)
**38** e.g. resident of Cairo (8)
**40** Caused by disease (12)
**43** Contents of the Mediterranean (8)
**47** Tradition (6)
**48** Insurance calculator (7)
**49** Scheme intended to deceive (3-2)
**50** Listening device (3)
**51** Blocks a decision (6)
**52** Confess to be true (5)
**53** Indigenous people (7)

## Down

**1** Capital of Cuba (6)
**2** Source of caviar (6)
**3** Arm muscle (6)
**4** Irrelevant pieces of information (6)
**5** Variety (9)
**6** Feeling of resentment or jealousy (4)
**7** Seaport in South Africa (6)
**8** Untimely (12)
**10** Based on a mistaken belief (10)
**11** Be alive; be real (5)
**16** Sulks (5)
**17** Coniferous tree (3)
**19** Ludicrous (9)
**21** Evidence of disease (7)
**22** Tentacled cephalopod (7)
**23** Scheming; acting deceitfully (9)
**25** Make ineffective (7)
**26** Inclination (7)
**29** Erase trumpet (anag.) (12)
**32** Expert advisor (10)
**35** Person who eats in a restaurant (5)
**36** Period without war (9)
**39** Animal foot (3)
**41** Sausage in a roll (3,3)
**42** Young sheep (5)
**43** Throwing at a target (6)
**44** Plus points (6)
**45** Opposite of passive (6)
**46** Reveal (6)
**48** Jelly or culture medium (4)

## *No. 56*

1 2 3 4 5 6 7 8
9 10 11
12
13 14 15
16 17 18 19
20 21 22 23 24 25 26
27
28 29 30
31 32
33 34 35
36
37 38 39
40 41 42 43 44 45 46
47 48 49
50
51 52 53

## No. 57

### Across

**9** Distribute again (11)
**10** Confine (8)
**12** Voracious marine fish (9)
**13** Computation (11)
**14** Immensity (8)
**16** Valuable thing (5)
**19** Detected a sound (5)
**20** Reprimanding (7-3)
**22** Forsaken (9)
**25** Clear mess away (5,2)
**28** Cattle-breeding farm (5)
**29** Small seat (5)
**30** Creative thoughts (5)
**31** Faint southern constellation (5)
**32** Excess (7)
**34** Unreserved in speech (9)
**36** Slightly unwell (10)
**38** Detection technology (5)
**40** Female relation (5)
**43** Base of a statue (8)
**45** Amazing (11)
**46** Periodical that is usually daily (9)
**47** Disloyal person (8)
**48** Streamlined (11)

### Down

**1** Decorative (10)
**2** District of a town in Spain (6)
**3** Style of speech (8)
**4** Passionate (6)
**5** Fillings (6)
**6** Prophet (6)
**7** Sandstone constituent (6)
**8** Made amends for (6)
**11** Discarded; binned (7)
**15** Becomes less severe (7)
**16** Agreeing with a request (11)
**17** Ceased developing (9)
**18** Instructs (7)
**21** Authoritative order (9)
**23** Loop with a running knot (5)
**24** Glazed earthenware (5)
**25** Capital of Egypt (5)
**26** Happening (5)
**27** Gourd-like squash (7)
**29** Earnest (7)
**33** A luxury (10)
**35** Spouse (7)
**37** How a crab moves (8)
**38** Country in central Africa (6)
**39** Hate (6)
**41** Exist permanently in (6)
**42** High-kicking dance (6)
**43** Outer part of a bird's wing (6)
**44** Emotional shock (6)

*No. 57*

## No. 58

### Across

**9** Taller and thinner (7)
**10** Plants of a region (5)
**11** Giggles (6)
**12** Wily (3)
**13** Aqualung (5)
**14** Juicy soft fruit (7)
**15** Equestrians (6)
**16** e.g. tennis (4,4)
**18** Altruism (12)
**20** Perfectly consistent (8)
**24** Violation of a law (10)
**27** Broaden (5)
**28** Song by two people (4)
**30** Large town (4)
**31** Effluence (7)
**32** Eyelet placed in a hole (7)
**33** Weapons (4)
**34** Blaze (4)
**36** Puff up (5)
**37** Corridor (10)
**38** Small telescope (8)
**40** Person studying after a first degree (12)
**43** Shows (8)
**47** Rousing from sleep (6)
**48** Painters (7)
**49** Move to music (5)
**50** Item of furniture one sleeps on (3)
**51** Drowsy (6)
**52** Compact (5)
**53** Voted in to office (7)

### Down

**1** State of matter (6)
**2** Straighten out (6)
**3** Large insect (6)
**4** Make (6)
**5** Ceramic material (9)
**6** The actors in a show (4)
**7** Heavy load (6)
**8** Marksman (12)
**10** Presage (10)
**11** Ancient harps (5)
**16** Beads (anag.) (5)
**17** Come together (3)
**19** Sea rescue vessels (9)
**21** Type of cell division (7)
**22** Going out (7)
**23** Believed (a lie) (9)
**25** Irregularity (7)
**26** Diplomatic (7)
**29** Not guided by good sense (12)
**32** Expression of surprise (8,2)
**35** Gets less difficult (5)
**36** Highly complex (9)
**39** Space or interval (3)
**41** Followed closely (6)
**42** Popular sport (5)
**43** Removed dirt from (6)
**44** Abrupt (6)
**45** Measurement of extent (6)
**46** Gives in (6)
**48** Sums together (4)

*No. 58*

*No. 59*

## Across

**9** A law forbidding something (11)
**10** State of the USA (8)
**12** Banishment from a group (9)
**13** Lacking distinguishing characteristics (11)
**14** Plan anew (8)
**16** Plant stalks (5)
**19** Harass; frustrate (5)
**20** Parochial (10)
**22** Lens used to direct light (9)
**25** Vending (7)
**28** Easily seen (11)
**30** Act of giving up one's job (11)
**31** Places of worship (7)
**33** Game bird (9)
**35** Container (10)
**37** Connection; link (3-2)
**39** Dreadful (5)
**42** Conduct business (8)
**44** Chance of happening (11)
**45** Uncultured; savage (9)
**46** Sticking together (8)
**47** Respectful (11)

## Down

**1** Punctuation mark (10)
**2** Made bitter (6)
**3** Glass-like volcanic rock (8)
**4** Part of a flower (6)
**5** Force fluid into (6)
**6** Cylindrical drum (3-3)
**7** Sincere; serious (6)
**8** Waterlogged (6)
**11** Mediocre (7)
**15** Desiring what someone else has (7)
**16** Restraint (4-7)
**17** Unconventional (of a person) (9)
**18** Type of quarry (7)
**21** Even though (2,5,2)
**23** Reel for winding yarn (5)
**24** Ascends (5)
**25** Sticky sweet liquid (5)
**26** Intense light beam (5)
**27** A parent's mother (7)
**29** Navigational instrument (7)
**32** In the end (10)
**34** Antlers (anag.) (7)
**36** Grasslands (8)
**37** Themes (6)
**38** Periods of history (6)
**40** Case for holding money (6)
**41** Messy (6)
**42** Pieces of furniture (6)
**43** Scared (6)

*No. 59*

1 2 3 4 5 6 7 8
9 10 11
12 13
14 15 16 17 18 19
20 21 22 23 24
25 26 27 28 29
30 31 32
33 34 35 36
37 38 39 40 41 42 43
44 45
46 47

*No. 60*

## Across

**1** Ukrainian port (6)
**5** Excitingly strange (6)
**8** Newsworthy (7)
**11** Facsimile (abbrev.) (3)
**12** State a belief confidently (6)
**13** Green vegetable (9)
**14** Tiny social insects (4)
**15** Business run jointly by its members (11)
**19** Person from another country (9)
**20** Unsafe structure (9)
**22** Unnecessarily (10)
**24** Devastating blow (6)
**25** Conceptually (13)
**31** The only remaining option (4,6)
**33** Make poor (10)
**36** Betrayer (6-7)
**40** A borough of New York City (6)
**42** Avoid committing oneself (10)
**45** Gravely (9)
**47** Speaking hesitantly (9)
**49** Unnecessary; superfluous (11)
**53** Luxurious car (abbrev.) (4)
**54** Case (9)
**55** Doctrines or beliefs (6)
**56** Wetland (3)
**57** Breaks (7)
**58** Local inhabitant (6)
**59** Pieces of writing (6)

## Down

**2** Undress (7)
**3** Cease being awake (5)
**4** Later (5)
**5** Precise (5)
**6** Part exchange for something new (5-2)
**7** Person employed to drive a car (9)
**8** Impartial (7)
**9** Inability to feel pain (9)
**10** Supple (5)
**16** Transitory (9)
**17** Surrounding glow (4)
**18** Data entered into a system (5)
**20** Lowed (anag.) (5)
**21** Accumulate (5)
**23** Parts of eggs (5)
**26** Dislikes intensely (5)
**27** Expect; think that (5)
**28** Catch sight of (4)
**29** Gullible (9)
**30** Ill-mannered person (4)
**32** Home (5)
**34** Individual things (5)
**35** Hurried (5)
**37** Generously given (9)
**38** Long-armed ape (9)
**39** Corrodes (5)
**41** Correct; accurate (4)
**43** Foreboding (7)
**44** Last in a series (7)
**46** Simple song for a baby (7)
**48** Self-evident truth (5)
**50** Explore or examine (5)
**51** Prod with the elbow (5)
**52** The protection of a particular person (5)

# *No. 60*

1 2 3 4 5 6 7 8 9 10
11
12 13 14
15 16 17 18 19
20 21 22 23
24 25 26 27 28 29
30
31 32 33 34 35
36 37 38 39 40
41
42 43 44 45 46
47 48 49 50 51 52
53 54 55
56
57 58 59

*No. 61*

## Across

**9** Seek out (6)
**11** Hawaiian greeting (5)
**13** Exceeds; surpasses (7)
**14** Climbing vine (3)
**15** Increase; extend (6)
**16** Capable of seeing (of a person) (7)
**17** Person who flies an aircraft (5)
**18** Imitator (12)
**20** Fortified wines (8)
**23** Comprehended (10)
**26** Apprehended (8)
**29** Gives out (5)
**30** In flower (6)
**31** Large heavy book (4)
**33** Strong desires (5)
**35** Excuse of any kind (5)
**36** Legume (4)
**37** Musician playing a double-reed instrument (6)
**38** Group of bees (5)
**40** Grammatical mistake (8)
**42** Expert on a subject (10)
**43** Stumbling (8)
**48** Heavy long-handled tool (12)
**51** Got to one's feet (5)
**52** Building (7)
**54** Sagacious (6)
**55** Louse egg (3)
**56** Has an impact on (7)
**57** Of definite shape (5)
**58** Desiring food (6)

## Down

**1** Resolvable (12)
**2** Multiply by three (6)
**3** 24 hour periods (4)
**4** Angular distance east or west (9)
**5** Donors (anag.) (6)
**6** Level plain without trees (6)
**7** Apprehend someone (6)
**8** Insect that transmits sleeping sickness (6)
**10** Tips (5)
**12** Continent round the South Pole (10)
**19** New word or phrase (9)
**21** Fish eggs (3)
**22** Move sideways (5)
**24** Enunciate (7)
**25** Japanese warrior (7)
**26** Apportioning (9)
**27** Pasta pockets (7)
**28** Take a seat (3,4)
**32** Mishap (12)
**34** UFOs (10)
**36** Attack on all sides (5)
**39** Fabrics (9)
**41** Container for a drink (3)
**44** Scoundrel (6)
**45** Trial impressions of pages (in printing) (6)
**46** Bring forth (6)
**47** Oily substance (6)
**49** Sandy wasteland (5)
**50** Insurrection (6)
**53** Ceases (4)

# *No. 61*

1 2 3 4 5 6 7 8
9 10 11 12 13
14
15 16 17
18 19 20 21 22
23 24 25 26 27 28
29
30 31 32
33 34 35
36 37
38 39
40 41 42
43 44 45 46 47 48 49 50
51 52 53 54
55
56 57 58

# *No. 62*

## Across

**9** Blocks of metal (6)
**11** Expressing emotions (of poetry) (5)
**13** Idealist; visionary (7)
**14** Deep hole in the ground (3)
**15** Treelike grass (6)
**16** Block (7)
**17** Once more (5)
**18** Compensate for (12)
**20** Dancing hall (8)
**23** Cocktail containing pineapple juice (4,6)
**26** Overcame (8)
**29** Assumed proposition (5)
**30** High-quality beef cuts (6)
**31** Spheres (4)
**33** Spoke softly (5)
**35** Signal assent with the head (3)
**36** Bitter-tasting substance (4)
**37** Toxin (6)
**38** Join together as one (5)
**40** Exclamation of surprise (8)
**42** Boat proprietors (10)
**43** Least old (8)
**48** Reckless; ready to react violently (7-5)
**51** Sink; sag (5)
**52** Moaned (7)
**54** Make a larger offer at auction (6)
**55** Tree of the genus Ulmus (3)
**56** Military person (7)
**57** Wise men (5)
**58** Marked by friendly companionship (6)

## Down

**1** Unfriendly (12)
**2** Cylinder holding thread (6)
**3** Singing voice (4)
**4** Feasible (9)
**5** Word that qualifies another (6)
**6** Remember (6)
**7** Make worse (6)
**8** Mustang; wild horse (6)
**10** Reproductive unit of fungi (5)
**12** Fellow national (10)
**19** Raised level surfaces (9)
**21** Allow (3)
**22** Fashions (5)
**24** Gave a prize (7)
**25** Vague and uncertain (7)
**26** Exasperating (9)
**27** Sign of the zodiac (7)
**28** Process of wearing away (7)
**32** Pertaining to a person's life (12)
**34** Discretion (anag.) (10)
**36** Irate (5)
**39** Act of spying (9)
**41** Annoy continuously (3)
**44** Strangest (6)
**45** Pasta strip (6)
**46** Quality of being lively (6)
**47** Large solitary cats (6)
**49** Chambers (5)
**50** Seek to hurt (6)
**53** Office table (4)

No. 62

1 2 3 4 5 6 7 8
9 10 11 12 13
14
15 16 17
18 19 20 21 22
23 24 25 26 27 28
29
30 31 32
33 34 35
36 37
38 39
40 41 42
43 44 45 46 47 48 49 50
51 52 53 54
55
56 57 58

## *No. 63*

### Across

**9** Substance that arouses desire (11)
**10** Person sent on a special mission (8)
**12** Benefit (9)
**13** Forewarning (11)
**14** Whole numbers (8)
**16** Follows orders (5)
**19** This date (5)
**20** Hits molars (anag.) (10)
**22** Stocks of money or other assets (9)
**25** Took the place of (7)
**28** Wash with water (5)
**29** Established custom (5)
**30** Make fun of someone (5)
**31** Sudden fear (5)
**32** Motorcycle attachment (7)
**34** Recalls (9)
**36** Fine details of something (3,3,4)
**38** Torn apart (5)
**40** Type of military operation (5)
**43** Beneficial (8)
**45** Very tall buildings (11)
**46** Absolve from blame (9)
**47** Official list of names (8)
**48** Nitrous oxide (8,3)

### Down

**1** Squeezes between two other things (10)
**2** Oppose a plan successfully (6)
**3** Adjoining (8)
**4** Rushes (anag.) (6)
**5** Dung beetle (6)
**6** Decorous; proper (6)
**7** Diverse (6)
**8** Capital of New South Wales (6)
**11** Massage technique (7)
**15** Surpass (7)
**16** Causing a blockage (11)
**17** Mistaken (9)
**18** Complex wholes (7)
**21** Recall past experiences (9)
**23** Having three dimensions (5)
**24** Indian lute (5)
**25** Speak (5)
**26** Deprive of weapons (5)
**27** Push down (7)
**29** Secret place (7)
**33** Unrestricted rule (10)
**35** Threatens (7)
**37** Overly anxious and sensitive (8)
**38** Popular holiday destination (6)
**39** Journey by sea (6)
**41** Deposit knowledge (6)
**42** Belt worn round the waist (6)
**43** Grow feathers (6)
**44** Rummage (6)

## *No. 63*

1 2 3 4 5 6 7 8
9 10 11
12 13
14 15 16 17 18 19
20 21 22 23 24
25 26 27 28 29
30 31 32 33
34 35 36 37
38 39 40 41 42 43 44
45 46
47 48

## No. 64

### Across

**9** Allowance given to children (6,5)
**10** Exclamation of joy (8)
**12** Study of the properties of sound (9)
**13** Compulsively (11)
**14** Longevity of an individual (8)
**16** Loud metallic sound (5)
**19** Colossus (5)
**20** Literary theft (10)
**22** Having regular lines and shapes (9)
**25** A deified mortal (7)
**28** State of having unlimited power (11)
**30** Greenish (11)
**31** Dullness (7)
**33** Wild with excitement (9)
**35** Covering with a thick layer (10)
**37** Making a knot in (5)
**39** Ridge (5)
**42** Make valid retrospectively (8)
**44** Temporary (11)
**45** Construct (9)
**46** Seahorse (anag.) (8)
**47** Act of copying (11)

### Down

**1** Destruction of the world (10)
**2** The back of the neck (6)
**3** Country in North East Africa (8)
**4** Child of your aunt or uncle (6)
**5** Token (6)
**6** Collapse (4,2)
**7** Least polite (6)
**8** Subatomic particle such as a nucleon (6)
**11** Letter (7)
**15** Pledged to marry (7)
**16** Free from financial concern (11)
**17** South American country (9)
**18** Gathered together (7)
**21** Became greater in size (9)
**23** Extent or limit (5)
**24** Strategic board game (5)
**25** Plummeted (5)
**26** Wall painting (5)
**27** Plunder (7)
**29** Enticed (7)
**32** Dividing into parts (10)
**34** Mischievous (7)
**36** Sudden forceful recoil (8)
**37** Computer keyboard user (6)
**38** Line of equal pressure on a map (6)
**40** Wore away gradually (6)
**41** Organs that secrete (6)
**42** Happen to (someone) (6)
**43** Very cold (of weather) (6)

## No. 64

1 2 3 4 5 6 7 8
9 10 11
12 13
14 15 16 17 18 19
20 21 22 23 24
25 26 27 28 29
30 31 32
33 34 35 36
37 38 39 40 41 42 43
44 45
46 47

*No. 65*

## Across

**1** Type of handicraft (7)
**5** Large wine bottle (6)
**8** Have a bad posture (6)
**11** Era (anag.) (3)
**12** Augury (4)
**13** Entertainingly (9)
**14** Black Sea peninsula (6)
**15** Row of trees (9)
**16** Impersonations (11)
**20** Inconclusive (10)
**21** Not embarrassed (9)
**24** Blandness (13)
**29** Mix socially (6)
**31** Restriction (10)
**33** Making more entertaining (10)
**35** Pygmy chimpanzee (6)
**36** Exaltation (13)
**40** Godless (9)
**42** Of the highest quality (5-5)
**44** Additionally (11)
**48** Be attracted to a person or thing (9)
**50** Summon; telephone (4-2)
**51** Venetian boatman (9)
**52** Deliberately taunt (4)
**53** 19th Greek letter (3)
**54** Organ (6)
**55** Legal practitioner (6)
**56** Secret agent (7)

## Down

**2** Lover of Juliet (5)
**3** Treaty (9)
**4** Kettledrums (7)
**5** Baffling stories (9)
**6** Sincere (7)
**7** District council head (5)
**8** Religious groups (5)
**9** Small antelope (5)
**10** Rid of something unpleasant (7)
**17** Blocks a hole (5)
**18** Energy and enthusiasm (4)
**19** Ongoing television serial (4,5)
**20** Adult insect (5)
**22** Capital of Vietnam (5)
**23** Remove errors from software (5)
**25** Set up or found (9)
**26** Revolve (4)
**27** Pertaining to birth (5)
**28** Besmirch (5)
**30** Musical staff sign (4)
**31** Venomous snake (5)
**32** A number between an eighth and a tenth (5)
**34** Sheltered places (5)
**36** Type of lizard (5)
**37** Asymmetrical (9)
**38** Easily controlled (9)
**39** Agitate (4)
**41** Type of natural disaster (7)
**42** e.g. Tuesday (7)
**43** Numbs (7)
**45** Bird claw (5)
**46** Not containing anything (5)
**47** Tycoon (5)
**49** Hackneyed (5)

# No. 65

1 2 3 4 5 6 7 8 9 10
11
12 13 14
15 16 17 18 19
20 21 22 23
24 25 26 27 28 29
30
31 32 33 34
35 36 37 38
39
40 41 42 43
44 45 46 47 48 49
50 51 52
53
54 55 56

*No. 66*

## Across

**9** Type of music (4,3,4)
**10** Religious deserter (8)
**12** Concerns; appeals (9)
**13** Creative (11)
**14** Rushing (2,1,5)
**16** Make a physical or mental effort (5)
**19** Embed; type of filling (5)
**20** Equivalent to (10)
**22** Initial (9)
**25** Collided with another vehicle (7)
**28** Not with anybody (5)
**29** Make less sharp (5)
**30** Sets of players (5)
**31** West Indian dance (5)
**32** Piercing cry (7)
**34** Contaminant (9)
**36** In a fairly quick tempo (of music) (10)
**38** Chubby (5)
**40** Evade (5)
**43** Thieves (8)
**45** Obvious (4-7)
**46** Robot (9)
**47** Relight a fire (8)
**48** Very vocal (4-7)

## Down

**1** Semiconductor device (10)
**2** Representation of a plan or theory (6)
**3** Very small unit of length (8)
**4** Of inferior quality (6)
**5** Peak (6)
**6** Cattle trough (6)
**7** Cosmetic treatment (6)
**8** Plant with edible stalks (6)
**11** Garnish (anag.) (7)
**15** Animal cages (7)
**16** Extend by inference (11)
**17** Newspaper opinion piece (9)
**18** Stock exchange workers (7)
**21** Boundless (9)
**23** Recycle (5)
**24** Gate fastener (5)
**25** Destroy (3,2)
**26** Use to one's advantage (5)
**27** Foolish person (7)
**29** Rod used in weightlifting (7)
**33** Point where a decision must be made (10)
**35** Indefinitely many (7)
**37** Whirling motion (8)
**38** Dough used for pies (6)
**39** Different from (6)
**41** Large quantity (6)
**42** Lightly (6)
**43** Trade names (6)
**44** Absence of passion (6)

# No. 66

1 2 3 4 5 6 7 8
9 10 11
12 13
14 15 16 17 18 19
20 21 22 23 24
25 26 27 28 29
30 31 32 33
34 35 36 37
38 39 40 41 42 43 44
45 46
47 48

## *No. 67*

### Across

**1** Bison (7)
**5** Part of the eye (6)
**8** Have an impact on (6)
**11** Father (3)
**12** Recedes (4)
**13** Sat with legs wide apart (9)
**14** Short trip to perform a task (6)
**15** Make a howling noise (9)
**16** Not absolute (11)
**20** Ability to do a thing well (10)
**21** Call (9)
**24** Splendidly (13)
**29** Out of breath (6)
**31** At all (10)
**33** Senior state or legal official (10)
**35** Set of steps (6)
**36** Mawkishly (13)
**40** Improving (9)
**42** Uncalled for (10)
**44** One who held a job previously (11)
**48** Enrage (9)
**50** Irrational fear (6)
**51** Commander (9)
**52** Chemical salt used in dyeing (4)
**53** Wager (3)
**54** Frightens; startles (6)
**55** Notable inconvenience (6)
**56** Robbers (7)

### Down

**2** Shadow (5)
**3** Angler (9)
**4** Social reject (7)
**5** Demanding situation (9)
**6** Embryonic root (7)
**7** Summed together (5)
**8** Very skilled at something (5)
**9** Relinquish (5)
**10** Have within (7)
**17** Crazy (5)
**18** Woes (4)
**19** Rash (9)
**20** Type of bus (5)
**22** Bits of meat of low value (5)
**23** Sea duck (5)
**25** Indemnity (9)
**26** Sparkling wine (4)
**27** Boldness; courage (5)
**28** Lawful (5)
**30** Tranquil (4)
**31** Use inefficiently (5)
**32** Embarrass (5)
**34** Stares at in a lecherous way (5)
**36** Road information boards (5)
**37** Lifeless (9)
**38** Detest (9)
**39** Heap (4)
**41** Small Arctic whale (7)
**42** Strange (anag.) (7)
**43** Candid (7)
**45** Prohibit (5)
**46** Decapod crustaceans (5)
**47** Metal worker (5)
**49** Armistice (5)

No. 67

1 2 3 4 5 6 7 8 9 10
11
12 13 14
15 16 17 18 19
20 21 22 23
24 25 26 27 28 29
30
31 32 33 34
35 36 37 38
39
40 41 42 43
44 45 46 47 48 49
50 51 52
53
54 55 56

## No. 68

### Across

**9** Approximations (11)
**10** Design engraved into a material (8)
**12** Six (4-5)
**13** Sea beacons (11)
**14** Married men (8)
**16** Boat (5)
**19** Exams (5)
**20** One who gives to a cause (10)
**22** Home (9)
**25** Type of computer (7)
**28** Strong ringing sound (5)
**29** Porcelain (5)
**30** Ironic metaphor (5)
**31** Exceed (5)
**32** Permit entry again (7)
**34** Athletic contest with ten events (9)
**36** Mild ghosts (anag.) (10)
**38** Yellow citrus fruit (5)
**40** In the middle of (5)
**43** Cosmetic product for the skin (8)
**45** Nostalgic (11)
**46** Urgent crisis (9)
**47** Mammal that chews the cud (8)
**48** Highest peak in Africa (11)

### Down

**1** Separable (10)
**2** Large sticks (6)
**3** Country in East Africa (8)
**4** Very tall mythical people (6)
**5** Aim to achieve something (6)
**6** To this place (literary) (6)
**7** Strong gusts of wind (6)
**8** Work chiefs (6)
**11** Disciple (7)
**15** Respire (7)
**16** Consideration of the future (11)
**17** Practice session for a performance (9)
**18** Less old (7)
**21** Opposite of relaxed (9)
**23** General hatred (5)
**24** Early version of a document (5)
**25** Showered with love (5)
**26** Indifferent to emotions (5)
**27** Dilemma (7)
**29** War trumpet (7)
**33** Teacher (10)
**35** Mental strain (7)
**37** Emaciated (8)
**38** Opposite of winners (6)
**39** Capital of Bahrain (6)
**41** Cause to start burning (6)
**42** Predatory marine fish (pl.) (6)
**43** Approval; recognition (6)
**44** Change rapidly from one position to another (6)

No. 68

1 2 3 4 5 6 7 8
9 10 11
12 13
14 15 16 17 18 19
20 21 22 23 24
25 26 27 28 29
30 31 32 33
34 35 36 37
38 39 40 41 42 43 44
45 46
47 48

*No. 69*

## Across

**9** Wind instrument (6)
**11** Lazed (5)
**13** A precise point in time (7)
**14** Edge of a cup (3)
**15** Large lizard (6)
**16** Ancient large storage jar (7)
**17** Perfect (5)
**18** Birds of prey (6,6)
**20** Effusion (8)
**23** Guidance; direction (10)
**26** Meddlesome person (8)
**29** Lance (5)
**30** Frolic (6)
**31** Pleasant (4)
**33** Assisted (5)
**35** State of disgrace (5)
**36** Hurl missiles at (4)
**37** Call something else (6)
**38** Recorded on video (5)
**40** Respite (8)
**42** Priceless (10)
**43** Social insect (8)
**48** Medicine taken when blocked-up (12)
**51** Do extremely well at (5)
**52** Solid inorganic substance (7)
**54** Self-evident truths (6)
**55** Be ill (3)
**56** Omission of a sound when speaking (7)
**57** Turn inside out (5)
**58** Fine cloth; type of paper (6)

## Down

**1** Bring together into a mass (12)
**2** Ahead (6)
**3** Capital of Peru (4)
**4** Casual footwear (4-5)
**5** Emperor of Japan (6)
**6** Support; help (6)
**7** Rich cake (6)
**8** Leaf stems (6)
**10** Instruct; teach (5)
**12** Sleepiness (10)
**19** Greek goddess of love (9)
**21** Purchase (3)
**22** Herb (5)
**24** Arguer (7)
**25** Fall back (7)
**26** Have profits that equal costs (5,4)
**27** More than two (7)
**28** A rich mine; big prize (7)
**32** Dark towering cloud (12)
**34** State of reliance (10)
**36** Roofed entrance to a house (5)
**39** Threw away (9)
**41** Very cold; slippery (3)
**44** Unwrapped (6)
**45** Greek mathematician (6)
**46** Sea in northern Europe (6)
**47** Expensive white fur (6)
**49** Praise highly (5)
**50** Desire for water (6)
**53** Thin strip of wood (4)

# *No. 69*

1 2 3 4 5 6 7 8
9 10 11 12 13
14
15 16 17
18 19 20 21 22
23 24 25 26 27 28
29
30 31 32
33 34 35
36 37
38 39
40 41 42
43 44 45 46 47 48 49 50
51 52 53 54
55
56 57 58

*No. 70*

## Across

**9** Form a mental picture (7)
**10** Cost (5)
**11** Calamitous (6)
**12** State of armed conflict (3)
**13** Open disrespect (5)
**14** Study of animals (7)
**15** Stimulate (6)
**16** Insincere and dishonest (3-5)
**18** Not familiar with or used to (12)
**20** Burns slightly or chars (8)
**24** Done in return (10)
**27** Greets with enthusiasm (5)
**28** Wander (4)
**30** Consumes food (4)
**31** Ardently; keenly (7)
**32** Not as tall (7)
**33** Pool (anag.) (4)
**34** Extent of a surface (4)
**36** Doctor (5)
**37** Capital of California (10)
**38** Limping (8)
**40** DIY stands for this (2-2-8)
**43** Raging conflagration (8)
**47** What a spider makes (6)
**48** Seats for more than one person (7)
**49** Of the nose (5)
**50** Not in (3)
**51** Cushion for the head (6)
**52** Explode (5)
**53** Foes (7)

## Down

**1** Puzzle composed of many pieces (6)
**2** Bribe (6)
**3** Meal eaten outdoors (6)
**4** Grabbed (6)
**5** Huge extinct animals (9)
**6** Wet with condensation (4)
**7** South American cowboy (6)
**8** Chatter (6-6)
**10** Depth of knowledge (10)
**11** Arduous journeys (5)
**16** Underground enlarged stem (5)
**17** Diving bird (3)
**19** Beetle-like insect (9)
**21** Climbing plant (7)
**22** Witty saying (7)
**23** Tool used when a pencil is blunt (9)
**25** Agitate (7)
**26** Generally; in summary (7)
**29** Use of words that mimic sounds (12)
**32** Secondary consequence of a drug (4,6)
**35** Standpoint (5)
**36** Of great significance (9)
**39** Of a low standard (3)
**41** Absorbent cloths (6)
**42** U-shaped curve in a river (5)
**43** Squandered (6)
**44** Horizontal supporting beam (6)
**45** Remains preserved in rock (6)
**46** Enjoy greatly (6)
**48** Proofreader's mark (4)

# No. 70

1 2 3 4 5 6 7 8
9 10 11
12
13 14 15
16 17 18 19
20 21 22 23 24 25 26
27
28 29 30
31 32
33 34 35
36
37 38 39
40 41 42 43 44 45 46
47 48 49
50
51 52 53

## No. 71

### Across

**1** Small cake (6)
**4** Applying to everything (6,3,5)
**10** Twelve (5)
**13** Act of checking the accuracy of an instrument (11)
**15** Receptacle for cigarette residue (7)
**17** Come together (8)
**19** Leave of absence (8)
**20** Omit (a sound) when speaking (5)
**23** Enormous (11)
**25** Deprive of power (6)
**26** Upper front part of a boot (4)
**28** Finished (5)
**29** Affectedness (15)
**32** Sound of a lion (4)
**34** A brief piece of film (4)
**36** Of low priority (2,3,4,6)
**40** Solid blow (5)
**41** Wingless jumping insect (4)
**42** Distinct being (6)
**43** Having celebrities in attendance (4-7)
**46** Escapade (5)
**48** Country in South East Asia (8)
**49** Remedy to a poison (8)
**51** Indulges a desire (7)
**53** Quality of being timeless (11)
**55** Awry; wrong (5)
**58** 1963 war epic starring Steve McQueen (3,5,6)
**59** Workroom of a painter (6)

### Down

**1** Deranged (3)
**2** Flat-topped conical hat (3)
**3** Public houses (4)
**4** Foreboding (12)
**5** Use again (7)
**6** Latin American dance (5)
**7** Key on a computer keyboard (3)
**8** Among (7)
**9** Washed lightly (6)
**11** Dweller (8)
**12** Soonest (8)
**14** Flower-shaped competition awards (8)
**16** Not quickly forgotten (8)
**18** Hate (6)
**21** Crowbar (5)
**22** Tallest species of penguin (7)
**24** Thrived (9)
**27** Furnish; decorate (5)
**29** Large ocean (7)
**30** Select group of people (5)
**31** Without parallel (6,2,4)
**33** Renounce or reject (8)
**35** Stage (5)
**36** Uses a piece of machinery (8)
**37** Inclined at an angle (6)
**38** Merciless (8)
**39** Twist together (8)
**44** Fishing boat (7)
**45** Type of diving (4-3)
**47** Join or fasten (6)
**50** Baking appliances (5)
**52** Speak in a wild way (4)
**54** e.g. use a chair (3)
**56** Child (3)
**57** How (anag.) (3)

# No. 71

## No. 72

### Across

**9** Unfasten (7)
**10** Hang with cloth (5)
**11** Middle Eastern language (6)
**12** Came first (3)
**13** Satisfied a desire (5)
**14** Large number (7)
**15** Sight (6)
**16** Core mass of a country (8)
**18** Annulment (12)
**20** Re-emerge (8)
**24** Up for debate (10)
**27** Choose through voting (5)
**28** Deceiver (4)
**30** Small body of water (4)
**31** State of disorder (7)
**32** Tenured (anag.) (7)
**33** Male deer (4)
**34** Chopped; cancelled (4)
**36** Manages (5)
**37** Extreme abundance (10)
**38** Astronaut (8)
**40** Fully extended (12)
**43** Inclination (8)
**47** Greek goddess of wisdom (6)
**48** Dressed in a vestment (7)
**49** Flexible insulated cables (5)
**50** Water barrier (3)
**51** Occurring every sixty minutes (6)
**52** Bring together (5)
**53** Ugly thing (7)

### Down

**1** World's largest country (6)
**2** Bleach (6)
**3** Sporting venues (6)
**4** Had corresponding sounds (6)
**5** Malevolent (9)
**6** Fastened with stitches (4)
**7** Breed of hound (6)
**8** Character in Mario Puzo's novel 'The Godfather' (4,8)
**10** Carefully and gently (10)
**11** Heavy iron block (5)
**16** Ethical (5)
**17** Cheek (slang) (3)
**19** Keenness (9)
**21** Model of excellence (7)
**22** Unpredictable (7)
**23** Floor covering rolled out for royalty (3,6)
**25** Mexican spirit (7)
**26** Satisfy; conciliate (7)
**29** Explanatory section of a book (12)
**32** Reliably (10)
**35** Fop (5)
**36** Purgation of emotions (9)
**39** Partly digested animal food (3)
**41** Smiles contemptuously (6)
**42** Fully prepared (5)
**43** Cleaned up (6)
**44** Cut slightly (6)
**45** Implant deeply (6)
**46** Type of nut (6)
**48** Flightless birds (4)

*No. 72*

1 2 3 4 5 6 7 8
9 10 11
12
13 14 15
16 17 18 19
20 21 22 23 24 25 26
27
28 29 30
31 32
33 34 35
36
37 38 39
40 41 42 43 44 45 46
47 48 49
50
51 52 53

*No. 73*

## Across

**9** Woman's garment (6)
**11** Tarns (anag.) (5)
**13** Pungent gas (7)
**14** Mouthpiece attached to a bridle (3)
**15** Plaster for coating walls (6)
**16** Uncomplaining (7)
**17** Foolishly credulous (5)
**18** State of the USA (12)
**20** Refer to famous people one knows (4-4)
**23** Small rodent (10)
**26** Progeny (8)
**29** Latin American dance (5)
**30** Avoiding waste; thrifty (6)
**31** Precious stones (4)
**33** Long rods (5)
**35** Strain (5)
**36** Endure (4)
**37** Culpable (6)
**38** Clean thoroughly; vegetation (5)
**40** Makes bigger (8)
**42** Probability (10)
**43** Lethargic (8)
**48** Gathering of people (12)
**51** Relating to a city (5)
**52** Breathed in sharply (7)
**54** Sloping (of a typeface) (6)
**55** Eccentric (3)
**56** Bizarre (7)
**57** Common seabirds (5)
**58** Background actors (6)

## Down

**1** Framework for washed garments (7,5)
**2** Roman god of fire (6)
**3** Creative disciplines (4)
**4** Someone who cannot sleep (9)
**5** Unit of volume (6)
**6** US rapper (6)
**7** Undone (6)
**8** Small summerhouse (6)
**10** Dark wood (5)
**12** e.g. baptism and matrimony (10)
**19** Worthless (9)
**21** Snake-like fish (3)
**22** Sudden sharp pains (5)
**24** Country in West Africa (7)
**25** Aiding (7)
**26** Person who looks after a building (9)
**27** Forbidden by law (7)
**28** Small shark (7)
**32** Based on legend (12)
**34** Scoring (10)
**36** Makes beer (5)
**39** Piece of cloth that covers the eyes (9)
**41** Floor mat (3)
**44** Migratory grasshopper (6)
**45** Rule with authority (6)
**46** Units of linear measure (6)
**47** Jostle (6)
**49** Move effortlessly through air (5)
**50** Attributes (6)
**53** Portion of medicine (4)

## *No. 73*

## No. 74

### Across

**1** Ordered (9)
**6** Fighting vessel (7)
**10** Hit high into the air (3)
**12** English Romantic poet who wrote the sonnet 'Ozymandias' (5,6,7)
**13** Steep and rugged rock (4)
**14** Speaks to an audience (9)
**16** A division between people (8)
**17** Possesses (4)
**18** Conventional (11)
**21** Easy victory (4-2)
**23** Be in debt (3)
**25** Dessert (anag.) (7)
**27** Eloquently (8)
**29** Writer of literary works (8)
**30** Self-contradictory statement (7)
**31** A desert in south-western Africa (8)
**33** Group of musicians (8)
**35** Featured in the leading role (7)
**38** Loud noise (3)
**39** Sharpening (6)
**40** Type of magician (11)
**42** Express a desire for (4)
**44** Substance used for polishing (8)
**46** Formula One race (5,4)
**48** Celebrity hero (4)
**49** Description of a fair situation (1,5,7,5)
**51** Appropriate (3)
**52** Graceful in form (7)
**53** Proposed an idea (9)

### Down

**1** Religious leader (6)
**2** Magnifying instrument (10)
**3** Aspiration (8)
**4** Far away (7)
**5** Remove water from (9)
**6** Saw (anag.) (3)
**7** Smells strongly (5)
**8** Grips (5)
**9** Study of the mind (10)
**11** Long for (5)
**15** Long poems derived from ancient tradition (5)
**19** Put in order (7)
**20** Hospital carers (6)
**22** The Netherlands (7)
**24** Fifth Greek letter (7)
**25** Computer keyboard users (7)
**26** Elevated step (5)
**28** Flowering plant with a prickly stem (6)
**32** Wipe out (10)
**34** Book written by hand (10)
**36** Preclude (5)
**37** Compels by coercion (9)
**39** Lecture forcefully (8)
**41** Moving along the ground (of aircraft) (7)
**43** Country in southern Asia (5)
**45** Hidden from view (6)
**46** Large waterbirds (5)
**47** Sporting stadium (5)
**50** Poker winnings (3)

## No. 74

1 2 3 4 5 6 7 8 9
10 11
12
13
14 15
16 17
18 19 20
21 22 23 24
25 26
27 28 29
30
31 32 33 34
35 36 37
38 39
40 41
42 43 44 45
46 47
48
49 50
51
52 53

## No. 75

### Across

**9** Template (7)
**10** Muscular tissue (5)
**11** Attack with severe criticism (6)
**12** Deviate off course (3)
**13** Punctuation mark (5)
**14** Acknowledgements (7)
**15** Becomes subject to (6)
**16** Classic US comedy TV series (8)
**18** Restore to good condition (12)
**20** Cyan tail (anag.) (8)
**24** Extortionate (10)
**27** Governed (5)
**28** Unit of type-size (4)
**30** Destroy (4)
**31** Repeats from memory (7)
**32** Someone who provides food (7)
**33** Total spread of a bridge (4)
**34** Helper (4)
**36** Longest river in Europe (5)
**37** Formal greeting (3,2,3,2)
**38** Protrudes (8)
**40** Highly abstract (12)
**43** Sleepily (8)
**47** Come off the tracks (6)
**48** Legislative bodies (7)
**49** Throw forcefully (5)
**50** Throat of a voracious animal (3)
**51** Relative social standing (6)
**52** Alter (5)
**53** Highest mountain (7)

### Down

**1** Soul; spirit (6)
**2** Sailor (6)
**3** Scratch (6)
**4** Cut up (6)
**5** Very pleased (9)
**6** Reasons; explanations (4)
**7** Surgical knife (6)
**8** Having an acrid wit (5-7)
**10** Heraldic lily (5-2-3)
**11** Flow with a whirling motion (5)
**16** Steep bank or slope (5)
**17** Cook in hot oil (3)
**19** Loop attached to footwear (9)
**21** Found out about (7)
**22** Densely (7)
**23** Literary analyses (9)
**25** Tortilla rolled around a filling (7)
**26** Patio or veranda (7)
**29** Enhancements (12)
**32** Deliberate (10)
**35** English homework assignment (5)
**36** e.g. Vesuvius and Etna (9)
**39** Chatter (3)
**41** Changes (6)
**42** Wheels that move rudders on ships (5)
**43** Banish; eliminate (6)
**44** Compensate for (6)
**45** Grins (6)
**46** Devices that illuminate (6)
**48** Moved through water (4)

## *No. 75*

1 2 3 4 5 6 7 8
9 10 11
12
13 14 15
16 17 18 19
20 21 22 23 24 25 26
27
28 29 30
31 32
33 34 35
36
37 38 39
40 41 42 43 44 45 46
47 48 49
50
51 52 53

## No. 76

### Across

**9** Creating an evocative mood (11)
**10** Away from land (8)
**12** Crescent-shaped pastry roll (9)
**13** Petty (5-6)
**14** Physically strong and active (8)
**16** Maladroit (5)
**19** Underground worker (5)
**20** Musical instrument (10)
**22** Dug up (9)
**25** Word having a similar meaning (7)
**28** Mimic (11)
**30** Word used by magicians (11)
**31** Insanity (7)
**33** Common garden herb (9)
**35** Entwine (10)
**37** Gardeners sow these (5)
**39** Radioactive gas (5)
**42** Glove (8)
**44** Business of entertaining visitors (11)
**45** Filled with wonder (9)
**46** A reduction in price (8)
**47** Link together (11)

### Down

**1** Society led by men (10)
**2** Mischievous (6)
**3** Scatter upon impact (8)
**4** Manic (6)
**5** Keen insight (6)
**6** Lump or blob (6)
**7** Capital of England (6)
**8** University lecturer (6)
**11** Glisten (7)
**15** Terse (7)
**16** Inventiveness (11)
**17** Kit; gear (9)
**18** A general proposition (7)
**21** Occupied (9)
**23** Lift with effort (5)
**24** Workers (5)
**25** Examines quickly (5)
**26** The Norwegian language (5)
**27** Dirtier (7)
**29** Remnant (7)
**32** Glasses (10)
**34** Revoke (7)
**36** Game of chance (8)
**37** Plan of action (6)
**38** Make certain of (6)
**40** In poor health (6)
**41** The science of light (6)
**42** Quick look (6)
**43** Immature insects (6)

*No. 76*

*No. 77*

## Across

**1** Floor covering (3)
**11** Speak very quietly (7)
**12** Former female pupil (6)
**13** Solemn promise (4)
**14** Toothed wheel (3)
**15** Statue of Jesus in Rio de Janeiro (6,3,8)
**16** Revival (7)
**18** Used a chair (3)
**20** Occurring in the absence of oxygen (9)
**22** Skilled worker (7)
**24** Joins together (5)
**25** Round building (7)
**26** Pestering constantly (7)
**27** Mixing together (11)
**33** Increasing gradually by degrees (11)
**36** Move apart (7)
**38** Illegally obtain money by deception (7)
**40** Overly sentimental (5)
**41** Act of going back in (2-5)
**42** Summary of religious doctrine (9)
**44** Place where one sees animals (3)
**46** Encode (7)
**48** Nicholas Evans' 1995 debut novel (3,5,9)
**50** Round bread roll (3)
**51** Finished; complete (4)
**52** Opposite of an acid (6)
**53** Letters (anag.) (7)
**54** Prevent (3)

## Down

**1** Fickle (9)
**2** Slender woody shoot (4)
**3** Claw (6)
**4** Uneasy (12)
**5** Comes up (6)
**6** Foolish (4)
**7** Words representing numbers (8)
**8** Garment passed from one person to another (4-2-4)
**9** Lively Spanish dance (6)
**10** Cheat someone financially (5-6)
**17** Pertaining to plants (7)
**19** Cloak (5)
**21** Disallow (3)
**23** Smooth transition (5)
**24** Ignite (5)
**28** Insanely (5)
**29** Animal lacking a backbone (12)
**30** Spiny yellow plant (5)
**31** Clumsily (7)
**32** Exoneration (11)
**34** Harmonica (5,5)
**35** City in Bolivia (2,3)
**37** Onlooker (9)
**39** In good health (3)
**40** To a certain extent (8)
**43** Urge (6)
**45** Argue against (6)
**47** Briefly; brusquely (6)
**49** Large wading bird (4)
**50** Sharp bristle (4)

## *No. 77*

1 2 3 4 5 6 7 8 9 10
11 12 13
14 15
16 17 18 19 20 21
22 23 24 25
26 27 28 29 30 31
32
33 34 35 36
37
38 39 40 41
42 43 44 45 46 47
48 49 50
51 52 53
54

## No. 78

### Across

**9** Choosing from various sources (8)
**11** Set a limit on (4,3,4)
**12** Thoughtful (11)
**13** Merchants who sell goods (9)
**14** Language of the Romans (5)
**15** Striped animal (5)
**18** Definite and clear (8)
**20** Blend (9)
**22** Inarticulate; muddled (10)
**24** Diaphanous (11)
**26** Morally right (7)
**29** Cunning (7)
**31** Think about carefully (11)
**32** Large kingfisher (10)
**34** Accuracy (9)
**36** Smallest unit of a compound (8)
**39** Produce as a fruit (5)
**42** Birds lay their eggs in these (5)
**45** Vigorous (9)
**46** Piece of software (11)
**47** Urging on (11)
**48** Proof of something (8)

### Down

**1** Writing implement (6)
**2** Celestial body (6)
**3** Rare (6)
**4** Newspaper boss (6)
**5** Change direction suddenly (6)
**6** Extreme audacity (8)
**7** Small boring tool (6)
**8** Fired clay (10)
**10** Italian red wine (7)
**15** Makes short and sharp turns (7)
**16** Apiarist (9)
**17** Highest class in society (11)
**19** Zeppelin (7)
**20** Gives as a reference (5)
**21** Fleshy (5)
**23** Customers collectively (9)
**25** Small spot (7)
**26** Green gemstone (7)
**27** Large wading bird (5)
**28** Lines (anag.) (5)
**30** Of similar opinion (4-6)
**33** Gusty (8)
**35** Drinking vessel (7)
**37** Song words (6)
**38** Coop up (6)
**40** Cast doubt upon (6)
**41** Drooped (6)
**43** Popular winter sport (6)
**44** Scorched (6)

## No. 78

1 2 3 4 5 6 7 8
9 10 11
12 13
14 15 16 17 18 19
20 21 22 23
24 25 26 27 28
29 30 31
32 33 34 35
36 37 38 39 40 41 42 43 44
45 46
47 48

*No. 79*

## Across

**1** Readying (7)
**5** Confronting and dealing with (6)
**8** Female sibling (6)
**11** Auction item (3)
**12** Biblical garden (4)
**13** Ridge of the Himalayas (9)
**14** Loves dearly (6)
**15** Self-assured (9)
**16** Small room that leads to a main one (11)
**20** Revival (10)
**21** Tiny molar (anag.) (9)
**24** Valetudinarian (13)
**29** Fix (6)
**31** Small keyboard instrument (10)
**33** Items of stationery (10)
**35** Small parrot (informal) (6)
**36** Respond aggressively to military action (7-6)
**40** Penniless (9)
**42** Deprive of property (10)
**44** Divisor (11)
**48** Pleasurable (9)
**50** Maiden (6)
**51** Occurrence (9)
**52** Fixes the result (4)
**53** Consume food (3)
**54** Enclosed recess (6)
**55** Hankers after (6)
**56** e.g. relating to touch or taste (7)

## Down

**2** Wireless (5)
**3** Public declaration of policy (9)
**4** Perennial plant with fleshy roots (7)
**5** Squashed (9)
**6** Bravery (7)
**7** Fit with glass (5)
**8** Secret store of something (5)
**9** Violent atmospheric disturbance (5)
**10** e.g. iron or oxygen (7)
**17** Invigorating medicine (5)
**18** Dairy product (4)
**19** Astonishment (9)
**20** Regal (5)
**22** Visual representation (5)
**23** Linear measures of three feet (5)
**25** Disapproval (9)
**26** Midday (4)
**27** Cowboy exhibition (5)
**28** Crime of setting something on fire (5)
**30** Movable barrier (4)
**31** Raised to the third power (5)
**32** Mountain range in South America (5)
**34** Moves back and forth (5)
**36** Fastening device (5)
**37** Insipid and bland (9)
**38** Book containing synonyms (9)
**39** Devastation (4)
**41** Look something over closely (7)
**42** Less clean (7)
**43** Opposes (7)
**45** Drives out from a place (5)
**46** Small piece of land (5)
**47** Friendship (5)
**49** Beer (5)

*No. 79*

1 2 3 4 5 6 7 8 9 10
11
12 13 14
15 16 17 18 19
20 21 22 23
24 25 26 27 28 29
30
31 32 33 34
35 36 37 38
39
40 41 42 43
44 45 46 47 48 49
50 51 52
53
54 55 56

# No. 80

## Across

**10** Left (6)
**11** Gigantic; huge (14)
**12** Freshwater game fish (4)
**13** Act of becoming apparent (9)
**15** Arch of the foot (6)
**16** Relieve or free from (3)
**17** Straighten out (6)
**19** Stanza of a poem (5)
**21** Making content (10)
**22** Solid ground (5,5)
**25** Young male (3)
**27** Fish appendage (3)
**29** Using both eyes (9)
**31** Not on (3)
**32** Bird of prey (6)
**34** Increase in amount (3)
**35** Sheep known for its wool (6)
**36** Craze (3)
**37** Stamina (9)
**38** Cereal grass (3)
**39** Measure of length (3)
**41** Likeness (10)
**43** Completely (10)
**46** Behaved (5)
**48** Surrender (6)
**50** Very small child (3)
**51** Cunning (6)
**53** Indispensable (9)
**55** Items that unlock doors (4)
**56** US author whose books include 'American Dirt' (7,7)
**57** A mother or father (6)

## Down

**1** Capable of being traded (12)
**2** Firmly fixed (6)
**3** Corner (4)
**4** Person who sees something (8)
**5** Faker (6)
**6** Inadequately manned (12)
**7** Interiors (7)
**8** Hens lay these (4)
**9** Mean sect (anag.) (8)
**14** Negative votes (4)
**18** Deserter (8)
**20** Something that is revealing (3-6)
**23** Performance (9)
**24** Wear away (6)
**26** Songlike cries (6)
**28** Low-cost travel package (2-6)
**30** Jail term without end (4,8)
**33** Very exciting (12)
**40** Detested (8)
**42** Most dirty (8)
**44** Undoing a knot (7)
**45** Ox-like mammals (4)
**47** Sport Andy Murray plays (6)
**49** Where bread is made (6)
**52** Ventilates (4)
**54** Circuits of a racetrack (4)

# *No. 80*

1 2 3 4 5 6 7 8 9
10 11
12 13 14 15
16
17 18 19 20
21
22 23 24
25 26 27 28
29 30 31 32 33
34
35 36 37
38 39
40 41 42
43 44 45
46 47 48 49
50
51 52 53 54 55
56 57

*No. 81*

## Across

**9** Compose a dance routine (11)
**10** Feeler (8)
**12** Aircraft device (9)
**13** Gymnastic devices (11)
**14** Unstable (8)
**16** Kick out (5)
**19** Undergarments (5)
**20** Destroy (10)
**22** Ambiguous (9)
**25** Taken as true (7)
**28** Gorge in Arizona (5,6)
**30** Curse (11)
**31** Moved round an axis (7)
**33** Converse (9)
**35** Component part (10)
**37** Celestial body (5)
**39** Legendary stories (5)
**42** Dour help (anag.) (8)
**44** Having good intentions (4-7)
**45** Symmetrical plane curves (9)
**46** Face-to-face conversation (3-2-3)
**47** State of preoccupation (11)

## Down

**1** Diligent and thorough (10)
**2** Jubilant (6)
**3** Extremely compatible partner (8)
**4** Attractive (6)
**5** Chest (6)
**6** Hinder the progress of (6)
**7** Parts of a play (6)
**8** Glasses contain these (6)
**11** Israeli city (3,4)
**15** Pared (7)
**16** Crises (11)
**17** Readying (9)
**18** Wash and iron (7)
**21** Building designer (9)
**23** Vault under a church (5)
**24** Covered the inside of a bin (5)
**25** Equipped (5)
**26** Grain storage chambers (5)
**27** Dignified conduct (7)
**29** Mound made by insects (7)
**32** Amuses (10)
**34** Piece of furniture (7)
**36** Extremely delicate (8)
**37** Cattle herder (6)
**38** Liquefied by heat (6)
**40** Over there (6)
**41** Aircraft housing (6)
**42** Self-important; arrogant (6)
**43** Visit informally (4,2)

*No. 81*

## No. 82

### Across

**9** Country in Central America (6)
**11** Foreign language (informal) (5)
**13** Organic solvent (7)
**14** Hog (3)
**15** Throw in the towel (4,2)
**16** Eternal (7)
**17** Prohibited by social custom (5)
**18** Study of the properties of moving air (12)
**20** Aromatic herb (8)
**23** Unimportant (10)
**26** Body movements that convey meaning (8)
**29** Mountain cry (5)
**30** Rough drawing (6)
**31** Large bodies of water (4)
**33** Solemn promises (5)
**35** Marry (3)
**36** Small drink of whisky (4)
**37** Moves very slowly (6)
**38** Lubricated (5)
**40** Polygon with five sides (8)
**42** Process of dying out (10)
**43** Atmospheric moisture (8)
**48** Impudence (12)
**51** Emits a breath of relief (5)
**52** Style of cooking (7)
**54** Of the eye (6)
**55** Male person (3)
**56** European country (7)
**57** You usually do this whilst asleep (5)
**58** Witches cast these (6)

### Down

**1** Skilled joiner (12)
**2** Get by with what is available (4,2)
**3** Simple non-flowering plant (4)
**4** Permanently (9)
**5** Sum of money demanded to release a captive (6)
**6** Trance (anag.) (6)
**7** Embarrassing mistake (3-3)
**8** Spanish title for a married woman (6)
**10** Put into use (5)
**12** Exceed in importance (10)
**19** Liveliness (9)
**21** Note down (3)
**22** Hides (5)
**24** Try (7)
**25** Reverberating (7)
**26** Fighter in ancient Rome (9)
**27** Semiconducting element (7)
**28** Brushed off the face (of hair) (7)
**32** Easy to converse with (12)
**34** Hardened (10)
**36** Extent (5)
**39** Felt hopeless (9)
**41** Additionally (3)
**44** Cause to fall from a horse (6)
**45** Take into the body (of food) (6)
**46** Place inside something else (6)
**47** Woody-stemmed plants (6)
**49** Golf clubs (5)
**50** Discharges (6)
**53** Prestigious TV award (4)

# No. 82

1 2 3 4 5 6 7 8
9 10 11 12 13
14
15 16 17
18 19 20 21 22
23 24 25 26 27 28
29
30 31 32
33 34 35
36 37
38 39
40 41 42
43 44 45 46 47 48 49 50
51 52 53 54
55
56 57 58

## *No. 83*

### Across

**1** By way of (3)
**11** Non-pedigree dog (7)
**12** Capital of Austria (6)
**13** Emperor of Rome 54-68 AD (4)
**14** Roll of bank notes (3)
**15** Leading British women's rights activist (8,9)
**16** Left out (7)
**18** Month (3)
**20** Intense type of pain (9)
**22** Fail to care for (7)
**24** Fire (5)
**25** Group of four (7)
**26** Introduced air to (7)
**27** Try to predict an outcome (6-5)
**33** Formal evening wear (6,5)
**36** Twist out of shape (7)
**38** Live together (7)
**40** Simple song (5)
**41** Back pain (7)
**42** Convert to another language (9)
**44** Increase the running speed of an engine (3)
**46** Last longer than (a rival) (7)
**48** Codename for the Battle of Normandy (9,8)
**50** Antelope (3)
**51** Yearn for; feel sore (4)
**52** Prayer (6)
**53** Flying vehicles without engines (7)
**54** Removed from sight (3)

### Down

**1** School of thought (9)
**2** Among (4)
**3** Turbulence (6)
**4** Planned in advance (12)
**5** Type of ski race (6)
**6** Flat and smooth (4)
**7** Retort (8)
**8** Information that sets the scene (10)
**9** Yearly (6)
**10** Type of artist (11)
**17** Firmly fix in a person (7)
**19** Resay (anag.) (5)
**21** Acquire (3)
**23** Strange and mysterious (5)
**24** Move out of the way (5)
**28** Overly self-confident (5)
**29** Not intoxicating (of a drink) (12)
**30** Darkness (5)
**31** Competitor (7)
**32** Serving to enlighten; instructive (11)
**34** Determination (10)
**35** Woodland spirit (5)
**37** Person providing protection (9)
**39** Seventh Greek letter (3)
**40** Profundity (8)
**43** Cared for (6)
**45** Fierce woman (6)
**47** Makes spick and span (6)
**49** Plant of the grape family (4)
**50** Lesion (4)

# *No. 83*

1 2 3 4 5 6 7 8 9 10
11 12 13
14 15
16 17 18 19 20 21
22 23 24 25
26 27 28 29 30 31
32
33 34 35 36
37
38 39 40 41
42 43 44 45 46 47
48 49 50
51 52 53
54

*No. 84*

## Across

**9** Study of lawbreaking (11)
**10** Arduous (8)
**12** Currently holding office (9)
**13** Orca (6,5)
**14** Muttered (8)
**16** Non-flowering plants (5)
**19** Beneath (5)
**20** Deep shade of blue (10)
**22** Reduced in length (9)
**25** Compliment unduly (7)
**28** Military constructions (5)
**29** Wild and untamed (5)
**30** Roman cloaks (5)
**31** Detailed assessment of accounts (5)
**32** Return to a former state (7)
**34** Mouth organ (9)
**36** Approximation (10)
**38** Length of interlaced hair (5)
**40** Units of heredity (5)
**43** Intelligentsia (8)
**45** Person who looks identical to another (6,5)
**46** Remained in effect (9)
**47** Someone paddling a light boat (8)
**48** Semi-transparent (11)

## Down

**1** Giving good value for money (10)
**2** Alcoholic drink (6)
**3** Whole; complete (8)
**4** Scolded strongly (6)
**5** Piece of text that names the writer of an article (6)
**6** Solent (anag.) (6)
**7** One who is easily frightened (6)
**8** Thin decorative coating (6)
**11** Civil action brought to court (7)
**15** Periods of 60 seconds (7)
**16** Ancestors (11)
**17** Self-control (9)
**18** Financial supporter (7)
**21** Introverted (9)
**23** Care for; look after (5)
**24** Model figures used as toys (5)
**25** Retrieve (5)
**26** Extreme displeasure (5)
**27** Harvesting (7)
**29** Pugilist (7)
**33** Views; opinions (10)
**35** Surpassed (7)
**37** Put into long-term storage (8)
**38** Light volcanic rock (6)
**39** Exposing one's views (6)
**41** Hostility (6)
**42** Next after seventh (6)
**43** Failing to win (6)
**44** Reply (6)

## No. 84

1 2 3 4 5 6 7 8

9 10 11

12 13

14 15 16 17 18 19

20 21 22 23 24

25 26 27 28 29

30 31 32 33

34 35 36 37

38 39 40 41 42 43 44

45 46

47 48

## No. 85

### Across

9 Like an eagle (8)
11 Substance applied to hair (11)
12 Traitorous (11)
13 Female rower (9)
14 One of the United Arab Emirates (5)
15 Smash into another vehicle (5)
18 Large rocks (8)
20 Faith systems (9)
22 Make inactive (10)
24 Membrane covering the front of the eye (11)
26 Hammers (7)
29 Walks leisurely (7)
31 Inconsistency (11)
32 Blowfly (10)
34 Welcoming; hospitable to outsiders (9)
36 Cold-blooded animals (8)
39 Japanese form of fencing (5)
42 Chocolate powder (5)
45 Leadership role in sport (9)
46 Act of rebuking severely (11)
47 Outer part of the earth (11)
48 Full of interesting happenings (8)

### Down

1 Sampled (food) (6)
2 Majestic (6)
3 Great fear (6)
4 Happens (6)
5 Boards (anag.) (6)
6 A magical quality (8)
7 A person in general (6)
8 Type of newspaper (10)
10 Wanting (7)
15 Options (7)
16 Attacker (9)
17 Children's game (4-3-4)
19 Bring to maturity (7)
20 Loose rugby scrums (5)
21 Passenger ship (5)
23 Attainment of a position (9)
25 Most unattractive (7)
26 Country in northwestern Africa (7)
27 Feeling of boredom (5)
28 Manner of writing (5)
30 Receptacle in a Church (10)
33 Greasiness (8)
35 Liberate; release (7)
37 Edible tuber (6)
38 Hay-cutting tool (6)
40 Avoids (6)
41 Hesitate (6)
43 Leaders (6)
44 Declares invalid (6)

*No. 85*

1 2 3 4 5 6 7 8 9 10 11 12 13 14 15 16 17 18 19 20 21 22 23 24 25 26 27 28 29 30 31 32 33 34 35 36 37 38 39 40 41 42 43 44 45 46 47 48

## No. 86

### Across

**1** Able to read minds (7)
**5** Foot levers (6)
**8** Measure of electrical current (6)
**11** Witch (3)
**12** Splendid display and ceremony (4)
**13** Reproduce (9)
**14** Money received (6)
**15** Jubilation (9)
**16** Not hurtful (11)
**20** Express in other words (10)
**21** A point of entry (9)
**24** A transient occurrence (5,2,3,3)
**29** Helps; benefits (6)
**31** Activist (10)
**33** Special rights (10)
**35** Indicate (6)
**36** Aggressive self-assurance (13)
**40** Obstruct a process (9)
**42** A rectangular space (10)
**44** Not wanted (11)
**48** Fruiting body of a fungus (9)
**50** Metrical foot (6)
**51** Hire plots (anag.) (9)
**52** At a distance (4)
**53** Wonder (3)
**54** Free from discord (6)
**55** Detects; feels (6)
**56** Illness (7)

### Down

**2** Coastline (5)
**3** Storage spaces (9)
**4** Value greatly (7)
**5** Lie detector (9)
**6** Mislead on purpose (7)
**7** Projecting horizontal ledge (5)
**8** Nimble (5)
**9** Written agreements (5)
**10** Act of getting rid of something (7)
**17** Many times (5)
**18** Eating implement (4)
**19** Capital of the state of Tennessee (9)
**20** Lively Bohemian dance (5)
**22** Outstanding (of a debt) (5)
**23** Work tables (5)
**25** Unfeeling (9)
**26** Musical or vocal sound (4)
**27** Acquires through merit (5)
**28** Plentiful (5)
**30** Public disturbance (4)
**31** Ciphers (5)
**32** Juicy fruit (5)
**34** Follow on from (5)
**36** Speak in public without preparation (2-3)
**37** Responses (9)
**38** Bad dream (9)
**39** Place where a wild animal lives (4)
**41** Tax imposed on ships (7)
**42** Questions (7)
**43** Cooked meat in the oven (7)
**45** Laud (5)
**46** Relative by marriage (2-3)
**47** Pains (5)
**49** Ellipses (5)

*No. 86*

## No. 87

### Across

**1** Soak up (6)
**5** Remove an obstruction from a sink (6)
**8** In the fresh air (7)
**11** Particle that is electrically charged (3)
**12** Banner or flag (6)
**13** Intoxicate (9)
**14** Hand over (4)
**15** Item that measures temperature (11)
**19** Administrative assistant (9)
**20** Having curative properties (9)
**22** Feeling of isolation (10)
**24** No one (6)
**25** Engaging (13)
**31** Supposition (10)
**33** Took away (10)
**36** Australian tennis player with 24 Grand Slam singles titles (8,5)
**40** Three times (6)
**42** Female opera star (5,5)
**45** Very pretty (9)
**47** Tropical fruit (9)
**49** Extremely steep (11)
**53** Indian garment (4)
**54** Lowest female singing voice (9)
**55** Legitimate (6)
**56** Also (3)
**57** Coatings (7)
**58** Disengage (6)
**59** Hold close (6)

### Down

**2** Female spirit (7)
**3** Willow twig (5)
**4** Game of chance (5)
**5** Join together (5)
**6** Open-minded; given freely (7)
**7** Continuous slide of musical notes (9)
**8** Relating to sight (7)
**9** Blind (9)
**10** Person who goes underwater (5)
**16** Tree known for the nut it produces (9)
**17** Fix (4)
**18** Spring flower (5)
**20** Spiritual nourishment (5)
**21** Moneys owed (5)
**23** e.g. taste or touch (5)
**26** Music with a recurrent theme (5)
**27** Show-off (5)
**28** Cries (4)
**29** Type of pasta (9)
**30** Fabric used to dress wounds (4)
**32** Impress a pattern on (5)
**34** Robber (5)
**35** Reside (5)
**37** Criterion directing action (9)
**38** Changed one's faith (9)
**39** Piece of furniture (5)
**41** Hired form of transport (4)
**43** Brings to effective action (7)
**44** Road or roofing material (7)
**46** Uncommon (7)
**48** Lacking meaning (5)
**50** Fabric (5)
**51** Large mast (5)
**52** Municipalities (5)

*No. 87*

1 2 3 4 5 6 7 8 9 10

11

12 13 14

15 16 17 18 19

20 21 22 23

24 25 26 27 28 29

30

31 32 33 34 35

36 37 38 39 40

41

42 43 44 45 46

47 48 49 50 51 52

53 54 55

56

57 58 59

*No. 88*

## Across

1 Form of public transport (3)
11 Cup (7)
12 Roe of sturgeon (6)
13 Slightly open (4)
14 Finish first (3)
15 Avoid coming to the point (4,6,3,4)
16 Art of paper-folding (7)
18 Sewn edge (3)
20 Study of signs and symbols (9)
22 Variety of rummy (7)
24 Tiny aquatic plants (5)
25 Verifier (7)
26 More spacious (7)
27 Specialist in care for the feet (11)
33 Free from control (11)
36 Release from captivity (3,4)
38 Render utterly perplexed (7)
40 Make amends (5)
41 Snuggles (7)
42 His refund (anag.) (9)
44 Dry (of wine) (3)
46 Capable of relieving pain (7)
48 Person who is good at talking (17)
50 Possessed (3)
51 Invalid (4)
52 Overseas (6)
53 Design of fashionable clothes (7)
54 Excavate (3)

## Down

1 Burner mixing air and gas (9)
2 Examine quickly (4)
3 11th Greek letter (6)
4 State of being in disrepair (12)
5 Angel of the highest order (6)
6 Repetition of a sound (4)
7 Fade away (8)
8 High-ranking cleric (10)
9 Burrowing long-eared mammal (6)
10 Coordinate (11)
17 Paid no attention to (7)
19 Supernatural skill (5)
21 Kind or sort (3)
23 Tread heavily (5)
24 Concur (5)
28 A point in question (5)
29 Intended to attract notice (12)
30 Unpleasant giants (5)
31 Perfectly (7)
32 Important (11)
34 Person who rides horses (10)
35 e.g. screwdrivers and hammers (5)
37 Going up (9)
39 Boolean operator (3)
40 Interview for an acting role (8)
43 Books (6)
45 Possibility (6)
47 Yield (6)
49 Betting figures (4)
50 Pay close attention to (4)

*No. 88*

1 2 3 4 5 6 7 8 9 10 11 12 13 14 15 16 17 18 19 20 21 22 23 24 25 26 27 28 29 30 31 32 33 34 35 36 37 38 39 40 41 42 43 44 45 46 47 48 49 50 51 52 53 54

*No. 89*

## Across

**9** Sharp cutting implements (6)
**11** Declares (5)
**13** Vacates (7)
**14** Pull at (3)
**15** Evening party (6)
**16** Protects from harm (7)
**17** Display freely (5)
**18** Irrelevant (12)
**20** Precludes (8)
**23** Temperature scale (10)
**26** Very small amount of money (8)
**29** Operate a motor vehicle (5)
**30** Expose (6)
**31** Extol (4)
**33** Inactive (5)
**35** Bite sharply (3)
**36** Remnant (4)
**37** Pertaining to the mind (6)
**38** Lingers furtively (5)
**40** Ritual (8)
**42** Dentifrice (10)
**43** Firmness (8)
**48** Vain (12)
**51** Lukewarm (5)
**52** Offence (7)
**54** Graphical representation of a person (6)
**55** Put down (3)
**56** Squeeze into a compact mass (7)
**57** Seven (anag.) (5)
**58** Crackle (6)

## Down

**1** Formal notice (12)
**2** Exaggerate (6)
**3** Pieces of cloth (4)
**4** Brought to a destination (9)
**5** Botch (4-2)
**6** Each (6)
**7** Body shape (6)
**8** Feature (6)
**10** Cooks slowly in liquid (5)
**12** Greeting (10)
**19** Issued every three months (9)
**21** Animal doctor (3)
**22** Warhorse (5)
**24** Quiver (7)
**25** US space probe to Jupiter (7)
**26** Spicy sausage (9)
**27** Victory (7)
**28** Capital of the US state of Georgia (7)
**32** Impossible to achieve (12)
**34** Able to be ended (10)
**36** Large bags (5)
**39** Astronomer (9)
**41** Wet soil (3)
**44** Slow to understand (6)
**45** Bring in from abroad (6)
**46** One of the halogens (6)
**47** Young people (6)
**49** Rocks back and forth (5)
**50** Attractive and stylish (6)
**53** Otherwise (4)

*No. 89*

*No. 90*

## Across

**10** Gastropods with shells (6)
**11** Location in San Francisco Bay with a prison (8,6)
**12** Obscures (4)
**13** Biologist studying the environment (9)
**15** Make illegal (6)
**16** Opposite of high (3)
**17** Incidental remarks (6)
**19** Grasslike marsh plant (5)
**21** Officer who administers the law (10)
**22** Very detailed (of an account) (4-2-4)
**25** Steal (3)
**27** e.g. Hedwig in Harry Potter (3)
**29** Eager and ready to fight (9)
**31** Thee (3)
**32** Republic once ruled by Idi Amin (6)
**34** Unit of current (3)
**35** Tyrant (6)
**36** Snip (3)
**37** Dependency on a substance (9)
**38** Large salt water body (3)
**39** Possesses (3)
**41** Complex; treacherous (10)
**43** Making a shrill sound (10)
**46** Living in a city (5)
**48** Scandinavian (6)
**50** University teacher (3)
**51** Helix (6)
**53** Understand (9)
**55** Fixes in place (4)
**56** Final track on Adele's '21' album (7,4,3)
**57** Pursue (6)

## Down

**1** Heartbroken (12)
**2** Not impartial (6)
**3** Land surrounded by water (4)
**4** Merry-go-round (8)
**5** Reverberated (6)
**6** Place of conflict (12)
**7** Refuses to acknowledge (7)
**8** Narrow opening; lits (anag.) (4)
**9** Madness (8)
**14** Single article (4)
**18** Hairdressers (8)
**20** One who writes plays (9)
**23** Self-control (9)
**24** Flowers arranged in a ring (6)
**26** Go around (6)
**28** Formal meal (8)
**30** Now and then (12)
**33** Condemnation (12)
**40** Person who shapes stone (8)
**42** Person in second place (6-2)
**44** Type of cooking apple (7)
**45** Swallow eagerly (4)
**47** Farewell remark (3-3)
**49** Fund-raising lottery (6)
**52** Long grass (4)
**54** Openly refuse to obey an order (4)

## No. 90

*No. 91*

## Across

**1** Children's book about a giant canine (8,3,3,3,3)
**10** Atlas page (3)
**11** Large indefinite amount (5)
**14** Device that measures electric current (7)
**15** Attack (7)
**16** Frenzied (5)
**17** What you hear with (3)
**18** More pleasant (5)
**21** Limb (3)
**22** Plain and clear (7)
**23** Act of extending by inference (13)
**25** Possess (3)
**27** Elucidated by using an example (11)
**30** Immortal (literary) (9)
**31** Deceives or misleads (5)
**33** Large number of people (9)
**35** Avoid (5)
**36** Truly (9)
**38** Act of making peace (11)
**42** Material from which a metal is extracted (3)
**43** Pertaining to building design (13)
**45** Walk with difficulty (7)
**48** Nevertheless (3)
**49** Russian sovereigns (5)
**52** Not new (3)
**53** Dull car sounds (5)
**55** Long pins (7)
**56** Mediterranean coastal region (7)
**57** Short choral composition (5)
**58** Pouch; enclosed space (3)
**59** Baroque composer of works such as 'Water Music' and 'Messiah' (6,8,6)

## Down

**1** Master of ceremonies (7)
**2** Fair (9)
**3** Abandon (7)
**4** Body that supervises an industry (9)
**5** Will (9)
**6** Bate (anag.) (4)
**7** Opposing political progress (11)
**8** Evil spirit (5)
**9** Diving waterbird (5)
**12** Extent (5)
**13** Division of the United Kingdom (7)
**19** Grotesque monster (7)
**20** Becoming popular once more (9)
**24** e.g. Usain Bolt (7)
**26** Cry with sorrow or grief (4)
**27** Angry (9)
**28** Japanese dish of raw fish (7)
**29** Stage play (5)
**32** Cure-all (7)
**33** Easily achieved (5,2,4)
**34** Rank (4)
**37** Chemical element with symbol Y (7)
**39** Synthetic fabric (9)
**40** Concerned with beauty (9)
**41** Totally absorbed by (9)
**44** Cook meat in the oven (5)
**46** Country in North Africa (7)
**47** Far-reaching; thorough (7)
**50** Move back and forth (5)
**51** Remove wool from sheep (5)
**54** Desert in northern China (4)

## No. 91

1 2 3 4 5 6 7 8 9
10 11 12 13 14
15 16
17 18 19 20
21
22 23 24
25 26
27 28 29 30
31 32 33 34 35
36 37 38 39 40 41
42
43 44 45 46 47
48
49 50 51 52
53 54 55
56 57 58
59

## No. 92

### Across

1 Bleat of a sheep (3)
11 Light-hearted (7)
12 Disdains (6)
13 Scottish singer-songwriter (4)
14 Was in first place (3)
15 Phrase that means both parties involved in a situation are responsible for it (2,5,3,2,5)
16 Larval frog (7)
18 Become firm (3)
20 Vexed (9)
22 Small bone in the ear (7)
24 Momentary oversight (5)
25 Feeling of vexation (7)
26 Identifying outfit (7)
27 Dismantle (11)
33 Needleworker (11)
36 Short musical composition (7)
38 Be given (7)
40 Rental agreement (5)
41 Framework (7)
42 Female ballet dancer (9)
44 Drink a little (3)
46 Iron attractors (7)
48 British-American actress from the Golden Age of Hollywood (6,2,9)
50 Evergreen coniferous tree (3)
51 Sight organs (4)
52 Small finch (6)
53 Sickness (7)
54 Plaything (3)

### Down

1 Container for voting slips (6,3)
2 Imitated (4)
3 Coarse cloth (6)
4 Unofficially (3,3,6)
5 Small pieces; slivers (6)
6 Employs (4)
7 American game bird (8)
8 Amazes (10)
9 Mammal related to the llama (6)
10 Lower in rank (11)
17 Move; agitate (7)
19 Used a computer keyboard (5)
21 Bitumen (3)
23 Cotton twill fabric (5)
24 Arboreal primate (5)
28 Hidden storage space (5)
29 Not catching fire easily (3-9)
30 Distinguishing characteristic (5)
31 Dissimilar (7)
32 Crushed with sorrow (11)
34 Changeless (10)
35 Highways (5)
37 Unhurried (9)
39 Mountain pass (3)
40 Hating (8)
43 Princely (6)
45 Insipid (6)
47 Ingenious device (6)
49 Block a decision (4)
50 Closed hand (4)

*No. 92*

## *No. 93*

### Across

**9** Unfortunate (11)
**10** Conceited (8)
**12** Derived from experience (9)
**13** Component part (11)
**14** Promontory (8)
**16** Strong thick rope (5)
**19** Saying (5)
**20** Record of heart activity (10)
**22** Easily angered (9)
**25** Made of clay hardened by heat (7)
**28** Landmark in Paris (6,5)
**30** Legendary transport device (5,6)
**31** Turns around (on a chair) (7)
**33** Card game for one (9)
**35** Device for regulating temperature (10)
**37** Kingdom (5)
**39** Thing that imparts motion (5)
**42** A period of 366 days (4,4)
**44** Dissatisfied (11)
**45** Thwart (9)
**46** Living thing (8)
**47** Car pedal (11)

### Down

**1** At first sight (5,5)
**2** Less attractive (6)
**3** Ascot cat (anag.) (8)
**4** Named (6)
**5** Soft felt hat (6)
**6** Adornment of hanging threads (6)
**7** Photographic equipment (6)
**8** Sculptured figure (6)
**11** Live longer than (7)
**15** Constantly present (7)
**16** Person describing a sports event (11)
**17** Business holdall (9)
**18** People who make money (7)
**21** Receiver (9)
**23** Single-edged hunting knife (5)
**24** Peers (5)
**25** Arrives (5)
**26** Royal (5)
**27** Skull (7)
**29** Parched (7)
**32** Written works (10)
**34** Marmoset (7)
**36** Calculated and careful (8)
**37** Extremely fashionable; scalding (3-3)
**38** Mete out (6)
**40** Top aim (anag.) (6)
**41** Musical dramas (6)
**42** Elevated off the ground (6)
**43** Printed mistakes (6)

## *No. 93*

1 2 3 4 5 6 7 8
9 10 11
12 13
14 15 16 17 18 19
20 21 22 23 24
25 26 27 28 29
30 31 32
33 34 35 36
37 38 39 40 41 42 43
44 45
46 47

## No. 94

### Across

**9** A long way away (3,3)
**11** Not illuminated (5)
**13** Distant settlement (7)
**14** Sharp blow (3)
**15** Ludicrous failure (6)
**16** Coming from the south (7)
**17** Made a mistake (5)
**18** Duplication (12)
**20** Booklet (8)
**23** Branched candlestick (10)
**26** Justified in terms of profitability (8)
**29** Shoe ties (5)
**30** Communal (6)
**31** Helps (4)
**33** Hankered after (5)
**35** People not ordained (5)
**36** Dejected (4)
**37** Iridaceous plants (6)
**38** Abatement (5)
**40** Sit with legs wide apart (8)
**42** Adversary; foe (10)
**43** Go past another car (8)
**48** Radishes grin (anag.) (12)
**51** Stiff (5)
**52** Immature fruit of a cucumber (7)
**54** Enter a country by force (6)
**55** Choose (3)
**56** Endless (7)
**57** Military vehicles (5)
**58** Small fasteners (6)

### Down

**1** Welsh fashion designer (5,7)
**2** Water diviner (6)
**3** Brass musical instrument (4)
**4** Genre of music (9)
**5** Move with a bounding motion (6)
**6** Body of running water (6)
**7** Next after third (6)
**8** Heavy food (6)
**10** Narrow sea inlet (5)
**12** Despotic (10)
**19** Small space (9)
**21** Tack (3)
**22** Mexican tortilla wraps (5)
**24** Difficult choice (7)
**25** Found (7)
**26** Approximated (9)
**27** Doing as one is told (7)
**28** Formal speech (7)
**32** Scolding (8-4)
**34** Separation (10)
**36** Enthusiasm (5)
**39** Getting anxious (9)
**41** Small spot (3)
**44** Stanzas (6)
**45** Having a rough surface (of terrain) (6)
**46** Summing together (6)
**47** Surround (6)
**49** Modifies (5)
**50** Harsh (6)
**53** Facial feature (4)

*No. 94*

*No. 95*

## Across

**1** Diagrammatic (9)
**6** Person whose name is not specified (2-3-2)
**10** Bed for a baby (3)
**12** English portrait and landscape painter (6,12)
**13** Light toboggan (4)
**14** Coiffure (9)
**16** Section of a train (8)
**17** Bend or coil (4)
**18** Having four right angles (of a shape) (11)
**21** Spoken form of communication (6)
**23** Small social insect (3)
**25** Accounts inspector (7)
**27** Leave the ground (of a space rocket) (5,3)
**29** Rigorous investigation (8)
**30** Blank page in a book (7)
**31** Sleep disorder (8)
**33** Insect trap (8)
**35** Concern; implicate (7)
**38** What a painter creates (3)
**39** Rides a bike (6)
**40** Enjoyable (11)
**42** Type of starch (4)
**44** A cephalopod (8)
**46** Seize the day (5,4)
**48** Platform leading out to sea (4)
**49** Song written and recorded in 1973 by Dolly Parton (1,4,6,4,3)
**51** Violate a law of God (3)
**52** Lubricated (7)
**53** Cherished (9)

## Down

**1** Huge desert in North Africa (6)
**2** Fast food items (10)
**3** Confused mixture (8)
**4** Instructor (7)
**5** Certain of something (9)
**6** Cry (3)
**7** Ordered arrangement (5)
**8** Tennis score (5)
**9** Mob rule (10)
**11** Big cat (5)
**15** Viewpoint or angle (5)
**19** Tall quadruped (7)
**20** Insanity (6)
**22** Cornmeal (7)
**24** Ancient war galley (7)
**25** Business matters (7)
**26** Ice dwelling (5)
**28** Elaborately adorned (6)
**32** Large expression of emotion (10)
**34** Person conducting a sale of lots (10)
**36** Edge or border (5)
**37** Grease (9)
**39** Careful (8)
**41** All together (2,5)
**43** Sour substances (5)
**45** Maintain a decision (6)
**46** Culinary herb (5)
**47** Tumbles (5)
**50** Protective cover (3)

*No. 95*

1 2 3 4 5 6 7 8 9
10 11
12
13
14 15
16 17
18 19 20
21 22 23 24
25 26
27 28 29
30
31 32 33 34
35 36 37
38 39
40 41
42 43 44 45
46 47
48
49 50
51
52 53

## No. 96

### Across

**9** Aircraft (pl.) (11)
**10** For all time (8)
**12** A vocal sound (9)
**13** Spookiness (11)
**14** Modify with new parts (8)
**16** Competed in a speed contest (5)
**19** Interior (5)
**20** Coded message (10)
**22** One who guides a ship (9)
**25** Taking part in a game (7)
**28** Unwillingly (11)
**30** Fit to be seen (11)
**31** Triangle with three unequal sides (7)
**33** Vanish (9)
**35** Eagerness (10)
**37** Dry red wine (5)
**39** Glasses (abbrev.) (5)
**42** Trivial deception (5,3)
**44** Gadget (11)
**45** Not inevitable (9)
**46** Italian cheese (8)
**47** Philosophical doctrine (11)

### Down

**1** Grandiloquent (10)
**2** ___ Einstein: famous physicist (6)
**3** Constant movement from side to side (2,3,3)
**4** Thoroughfare (6)
**5** Respiratory condition (6)
**6** Person to whom a lease is granted (6)
**7** Meet or find by chance (4,2)
**8** Moral guardian (6)
**11** Lifting up (7)
**15** Cold-blooded vertebrate like a crocodile (7)
**16** Without guilt (11)
**17** Flowing together (9)
**18** Gadgets (7)
**21** Refund (9)
**23** Levy (5)
**24** Verse (5)
**25** Supplied by tube (5)
**26** Assists in a crime (5)
**27** Groups together (7)
**29** Greed (7)
**32** Pen name (3,2,5)
**34** Open area of grassland (7)
**36** Specified work outfits (8)
**37** List of ingredients for a dish (6)
**38** Possessors (6)
**40** Surface film; coating (6)
**41** Indistinct (6)
**42** Drove erratically (6)
**43** Introduction (4-2)

# No. 96

1 2 3 4 5 6 7 8 9 10 11 12 13 14 15 16 17 18 19 20 21 22 23 24 25 26 27 28 29 30 31 32 33 34 35 36 37 38 39 40 41 42 43 44 45 46 47

*No. 97*

**Across**

**1** Conciliatory gift (3)
**11** Not tense (7)
**12** Atmospheric phenomenon (6)
**13** Related by blood (4)
**14** Unit of energy (3)
**15** George R. R. Martin's epic fantasy book series (1,4,2,3,3,4)
**16** Prepare for printing (7)
**18** Viscous liquid (3)
**20** Floods (9)
**22** Stipulation (7)
**24** ___ O'Brien: US TV host and comedian (5)
**25** Crisp plain fabric (7)
**26** Praise strongly (7)
**27** Founded (11)
**33** Happenings (11)
**36** Player of an instrument that is low in pitch (7)
**38** Highest (7)
**40** Interruption (5)
**41** Fully occupy (7)
**42** Honesty; probity (9)
**44** Thing that fails to work properly (3)
**46** Routers (anag.) (7)
**48** 2006 TV film starring Zac Efron and Vanessa Hudgens (4,6,7)
**50** Wetland (3)
**51** Gospel writer (4)
**52** Agree or correspond (6)
**53** Cunning (7)
**54** Division of a play (3)

**Down**

**1** Dodges (9)
**2** Self-righteous person (4)
**3** Makes a weak cry (of sheep) (6)
**4** Exorbitant (12)
**5** In slow time (of music) (6)
**6** Young cow (4)
**7** Force of resistance; abrasion (8)
**8** Heavy projectile (10)
**9** Type of palm tree (6)
**10** Comprehends (11)
**17** Mundane (7)
**19** Sudden movement (5)
**21** Definite article (3)
**23** Bring on oneself (5)
**24** Comedian (5)
**28** Domestic cat (5)
**29** Wearing glasses (12)
**30** Cake decoration (5)
**31** Sausages in bread rolls (3,4)
**32** Every two weeks (11)
**34** Limited in extent (10)
**35** Dish of mixed vegetables (5)
**37** Person engaged in spaceflight (9)
**39** Place (3)
**40** Routine and ordinary (3-2-3)
**43** Sound reflections (6)
**45** Discontinuance; neglect (6)
**47** Constrain or compel (6)
**49** Manner or appearance (4)
**50** Greek cheese (4)

# No. 97

1 2 3 4 5 6 7 8 9 10
11 12 13
14 15
16 17 18 19 20 21
22 23 24 25
26 27 28 29 30 31
32
33 34 35 36
37
38 39 40 41
42 43 44 45 46 47
48 49 50
51 52 53
54

## No. 98

### Across

**1** Gilbert and Sullivan comic opera (3,7,2,8)
**10** Small amount of something (3)
**11** Feeling pleased and satisfied (5)
**14** Nine-sided shape (7)
**15** Newtlike salamander (7)
**16** Hard and brittle (5)
**17** Belonging to us (3)
**18** Clean with a brush (5)
**21** Religious sister (3)
**22** Least fresh (7)
**23** Fitness to fly (13)
**25** Finish (3)
**27** Insubordinate (11)
**30** Violate (9)
**31** Speed music is played at (5)
**33** Member of the Christian clergy (9)
**35** Requirements (5)
**36** Receptacle (9)
**38** Moved to another place (11)
**42** Touch gently (3)
**43** Untrustworthy (13)
**45** Ways of doing things (7)
**48** 17th Greek letter (3)
**49** Distinguishing character (5)
**52** Male sheep (3)
**53** Narcotics (5)
**55** Sheer dress fabric (7)
**56** Interim (anag.) (7)
**57** Antelope (5)
**58** Word expressing negation (3)
**59** Judith Kerr's tale about an unusual household visitor (3,5,3,4,2,3)

### Down

**1** Tiresome (7)
**2** Cause to feel self-conscious (9)
**3** Type of bill (7)
**4** Designated (of a time) (9)
**5** Seaside promenade (9)
**6** Number after three (4)
**7** Neutral (11)
**8** Female relatives (5)
**9** Bring to the conscious mind (5)
**12** Take place (5)
**13** Very hard form of carbon (7)
**19** Lift up (7)
**20** Owned (9)
**24** Fragrant gum or spice (7)
**26** Near (4)
**27** Investigator (9)
**28** Total weight of organisms (7)
**29** Implied (5)
**32** Sovereign (7)
**33** Astonishing (11)
**34** ___ Kendrick: US actress (4)
**37** Remains (7)
**39** Irregular (9)
**40** Use violence against (6-3)
**41** Dutch painter (9)
**44** Strong lightweight wood (5)
**46** Flexible athlete (7)
**47** Large island of Indonesia (7)
**50** Special reward (5)
**51** Holy person (5)
**54** Emit light (4)

*No. 98*

1 2 3 4 5 6 7 8 9
10 11 12 13 14
15 16
17 18 19 20
21
22 23 24
25 26
27 28 29 30
31 32 33 34 35
36 37 38 39 40 41
42
43 44 45 46 47
48
49 50 51 52
53 54 55
56 57 58
59

*No. 99*

## Across

**9** Sufficient (6)
**11** Tests (5)
**13** Critical (7)
**14** Half of two (3)
**15** Equine sounds (6)
**16** Deflect light (7)
**17** Big cats (5)
**18** Made (12)
**20** Hairstyle (8)
**23** From beginning to end (10)
**26** Betting (8)
**29** Port-au-Prince is the capital here (5)
**30** Breakfast food (6)
**31** Teeth holders (4)
**33** Sweet-scented shrub (5)
**35** Sign of the zodiac (5)
**36** Rip up (4)
**37** Organ in the mouth of a mammal (6)
**38** Give a solemn oath (5)
**40** Ringing in the ears (8)
**42** Institution of learning (10)
**43** Give courage (8)
**48** Devoted to music (12)
**51** Metal spikes with broadened heads (5)
**52** The Windy City (7)
**54** Metamorphic rock (6)
**55** Obtained (3)
**56** Commendation (7)
**57** Sum; add up (5)
**58** Walked quickly (6)

## Down

**1** Perform below expectation (12)
**2** Martial art (4,2)
**3** Cry of derision (4)
**4** Deceptive statement (4-5)
**5** Pertaining to vinegar (6)
**6** Central parts of cells (6)
**7** Inside information (3-3)
**8** Nearer (6)
**10** Plantain lily (5)
**12** Halt (10)
**19** Lacking force (9)
**21** Lie (3)
**22** Borders (5)
**24** Conquered by force (7)
**25** Chivalrous (7)
**26** Nonsense (9)
**27** Plant-eating aquatic mammal (7)
**28** Ions that bond to metal atoms (7)
**32** Hillside (12)
**34** Barrier at a border (10)
**36** Name of a book (5)
**39** Contemplative people (9)
**41** Unwell (3)
**44** Sixty seconds (6)
**45** Starting point (6)
**46** Item thrown by an athlete (6)
**47** Five cent coin (US) (6)
**49** Takes a break (5)
**50** Throes (anag.) (6)
**53** Look at amorously (4)

*No. 99*

1 2 3 4 5 6 7 8
9 10 11 12 13
14
15 16 17
18 19 20 21 22
23 24 25 26 27 28
29
30 31 32
33 34 35
36 37
38 39
40 41 42
43 44 45 46 47 48 49 50
51 52 53 54
55
56 57 58

## No. 100

### Across

**9** Although (6)
**11** About (5)
**13** Absolutely incredible (7)
**14** Flightless bird (3)
**15** Reactive metal (6)
**16** Terms of office (7)
**17** Single piece of information (5)
**18** Connection or association (12)
**20** Face up to a problem (8)
**23** Shape with eight plane faces (10)
**26** Cornerstone (8)
**29** Leg bone (5)
**30** Contributes information (6)
**31** One of the seven deadly sins (4)
**33** Observed (5)
**35** Mixture of gases we breathe (3)
**36** Dispatched (4)
**37** Unless (6)
**38** Panorama (5)
**40** Separate and distinct (8)
**42** Disparaging (10)
**43** Gibberish (8)
**48** Relating to numeric calculations (12)
**51** Show triumphant joy (5)
**52** Reduce expenditure (3,4)
**54** Call on (6)
**55** Item for catching fish (3)
**56** Less heavy (7)
**57** Research deeply (5)
**58** Squirt (6)

### Down

**1** Fence closure (anag.) (12)
**2** Part of the eye (6)
**3** Short tail (4)
**4** Cutting; incisive (9)
**5** Unit of astronomical length (6)
**6** Deprive of force (6)
**7** Notebook (6)
**8** Mythical male sea creatures (6)
**10** Musical speeds (5)
**12** Fear of heights (10)
**19** Spoken or written account of events (9)
**21** Enjoyable (3)
**22** Secret rendezvous (5)
**24** Living in water (7)
**25** Entrap (7)
**26** Female head of a family (9)
**27** Floating mass of frozen water (7)
**28** Ask for; try to obtain (7)
**32** Large grocery stores (12)
**34** Unable to concentrate (10)
**36** Danes (anag.) (5)
**39** Deserving respect (9)
**41** Herb (3)
**44** Frankly (6)
**45** Thick wet mud (6)
**46** Write a music score (6)
**47** Repeat performance (6)
**49** Leaves (5)
**50** Turn upside down (6)
**53** Leg joint (4)

*No. 100*

1 2 3 4 5 6 7 8
9 10 11 12 13
14
15 16 17
18 19 20 21 22
23 24 25 26 27 28
29
30 31 32
33 34 35
36 37
38 39
40 41 42
43 44 45 46 47 48 49 50
51 52 53 54
55
56 57 58

# Solutions

*No. 1*

| M | I | S | H | A | P | S |   | A | L | I | G | N | S |   | S | U | B | W | A | Y |
|---|---|---|---|---|---|---|---|---|---|---|---|---|---|---|---|---|---|---|---|---|
|   | N |   | E |   |   | T |   | G |   | S |   |   | P | I | P |   | E |   | U |   |
| I | D | E | A |   | R | E | G | R | E | T | F | U | L |   | E | N | T | E | R | S |
|   | E |   | D |   |   | W |   | E |   | H |   |   | A |   | L |   | E |   | I |   |
| E | X | P | L | I | C | A | T | E |   | M | E | N | T | A | L | B | L | O | C | K |
|   |   |   | I |   |   | R |   | M |   | U |   | E |   | C |   | I |   |   | L |   |
|   | F | A | N | C | Y | D | R | E | S | S |   | A | N | T | I | P | O | D | E | S |
|   | I |   | E |   |   |   |   | N |   |   |   | R |   | S |   | A |   | I |   | E |
| U | N | P | R | E | T | E | N | T | I | O | U | S |   |   | P | R | I | S | O | N |
|   | E |   |   | G |   |   | O |   | N |   | N |   | T |   |   | T |   | C |   | D |
| A | R | T | N | O | U | V | E | A | U |   | F | O | R | T | U | I | T | O | U | S |
| X |   | H |   | T |   |   | L |   | R |   | I |   | E |   |   | T |   |   | S |   |
| I | R | O | N | I | C |   |   | F | E | A | T | H | E | R | W | E | I | G | H | T |
| N |   | S |   | S |   | W |   | L |   |   |   | O |   |   |   |   | N |   | E |   |
| G | R | E | A | T | D | A | N | E |   | C | O | M | P | E | T | I | T | O | R |   |
|   | U |   |   | I |   | R |   | E |   | A |   | E |   | F |   |   | R |   |   |   |
| E | M | A | N | C | I | P | A | T | E | D |   | S | A | F | E | G | U | A | R | D |
|   | B |   | E |   | M |   | O |   |   | D |   | T |   | E |   |   | S |   | E |   |
| B | L | O | W | U | P |   | R | E | T | I | C | E | N | C | E |   | I | B | E | X |
|   | E |   | E |   | E | F | T |   |   | S |   | A |   | T |   |   | V |   | V |   |
| A | S | T | R | A | L |   | A | R | C | H | E | D |   | S | W | E | E | T | E | R |

*No. 2*

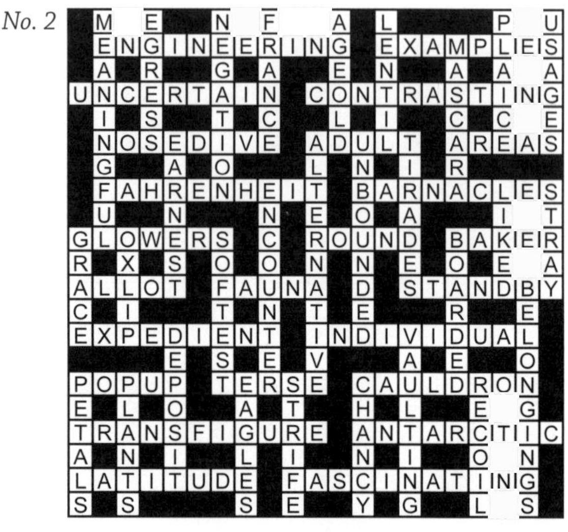

*No. 3*

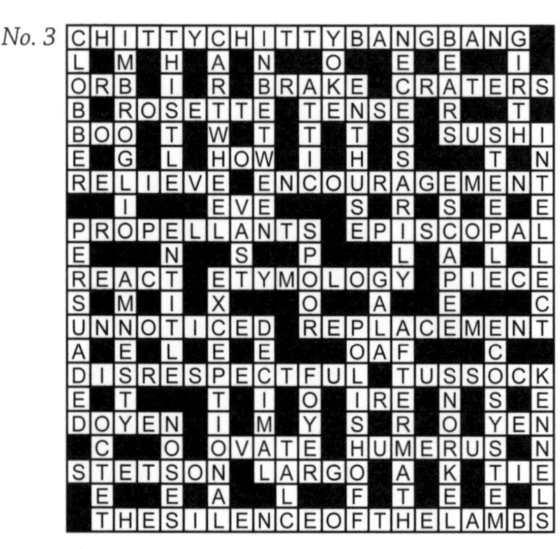

*No. 4*

*No. 5*

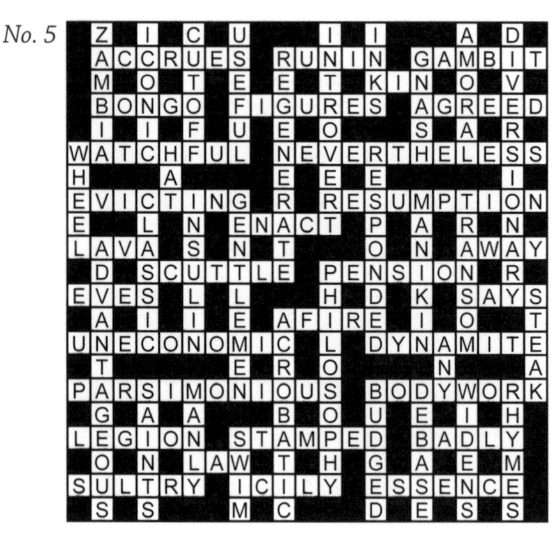

*No. 6*

*No. 7*

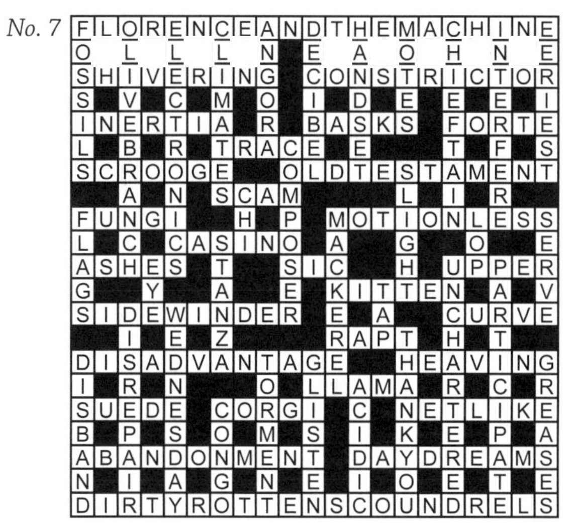


*No. 8*

*No. 9*

*No. 10*

COW P C C S P G S M
A HARMONY NEEDLE IDLE
R E E N G I R T E A
DAY SAVINGPRIVATERYAN
B E A E O H R I
ORBITAL TON DODECAGON
A I E O I C U G
RETINAS OPTIC CHATTEL
D U I C T E O E
MACBETH SCRUMPTIOUS
A E H N E O I O B S
CONJECTURAL GENERAL
C O E U D S O S
LEPTONS VOGUE BROWNIE
A U S I A O G N
MONUMENTS LOW GRASSES
A N C I H G S A
THEWAROFTHEWORLDS BAT
I E A O D L I A A I
ORAL TORRID LENDING O
N L E S Y Y G L SON

*No. 11*

*No. 12*

SCREED WARMER TONSURE
A D OAR I E O E E
TRYING ENCLOSURE PAIL
I C M S I E O A G
ABSTRACTART RENDERING
O E O D I V T A
DUMBFOUND APOLOGETIC
O O U P E I E E
MEMORY REMORSELESSLY
E O B B G R U L L
STATIONERY DECAHEDRON
H S A P E H C E A
CUTTHEMUSTARD STAVES
M H Q E S O E T
BREADCRUMB LITERALLY
R A I E T I A I
SUPERSTAR QUARRELSOME
S F I R U U T C P
SUMO SOVEREIGN UNUSED
R R N L S GAD F T
SPHERES SITUPS EFFUSE

## No. 13

E T A L E D D R
SCHERZO MAGMA UNEVEN
C R R O U Y ZEN T A
AROSE SYNAPSE TROOPS
P N S E I T I U P
HEIGHTEN FAINTHEARTED
O A I A H A
PENUMBRA C NEEDLEWORK
E P A FEEDS R E H A
SANG N F N E T OINK
L RINGLET TRUSTEE C
ULNA E U R P E VEER
I D R E AMIGO R E O
IMPERSONAL A NOSTRILS
P C L N E E
HOUSEKEEPING REUNIONS
R I N G U E N M E
STIGMA ENABLES COPRA
A N VAT T A U O A R
ENRAGE CHOIR LYRICAL
T L H R T K T Y

## No. 14

I E A L T A B G
ENSUES CLIMB URUGUAY
V R CUE P R R T R R
CUPOLA SESSION HYENA
L P L T D U O A T
INTERPRETIVE PERJURED
E X C G U O
CROSSCHECK R WESTWARD
A H O M SLOTH U A O
OBTAIN P O I C KISS
L C VALET MIMIC E U
BECK E I E S UNFURL
E L N FOLIO I M P
RECENTLY E VOCABULARY
T O S E A I
HEREWITH CARELESSNESS
N X M I O J H A I
ALPHA DIPLOMA INSANE
B A G I E Y PAN S G
LANTERN SCENE YEARLY
E D S G D X U Y

## No. 15

F S W K I R D S
OCCUPATIONS HYSTERIA
O H N S R Y E A W
ATTITUDES CARTOGRAPHY
B S E E E H N E E
RAMPARTS PLUMS ALDER
I A E R N T R
DIDGERIDOO READYMADE
G E I G E M P N
GERMANS S REFRIGERATE
A A N T P E I N X C M
BRITTLENESS N ALCHEMY
L S R R S E U I
ELEPHANTS INDECISION
U U A V L E D
PSALM MELEE SWINDLER
A D D J N T N E E
CAMARADERIE YACHTSMAN
I I U C G L H S D
FOREMOST MAKEBELIEVE
Y E S A D R R R

## No. 16

I T S F W S R T
INMOST IDOLS ANATOMY
C M RAG R T L D C C
SONATA NATURAL DUOMO
H T Y N O O E C O
REPOSSESSION PINPOINT
R O G G E H
HENCEFORTH H DECREASE
N L U C TROVE A M R
STROLL E L M S ONCE
L S SCRAP DRY S T A
LYRE O E E S ALIENS
I T M SURFS T V V T
PLASTERS I TRILATERAL
I I P I F N
DEDUCING HAPPYGOLUCKY
N N S A E U U N E
CHILL GORILLA TAPIRS
O Q A G A A VIE A O
DIURNAL LATTE RECOUP
E E D E E R K S

## No. 17

E R G A A C S S D
AMOEBA BENICIODELTORO
B M F L I N C O E
DATA FRAGMENTS REPOSE
R K T A O ICE S
BREEZE INLET D C T E
A V V EVERYWHERE
ESCAPEMENT R R S
S N N RIP AIDE E
INCENTIVE RIB INSIDE
N H E N MOO L L H I
IGLOOS AGO NEEDINESS
R SAD RUT G R I
P A M OPPRESSING
PRAGMATICS E N G
O E N S EASED TRAVEL
V YES L P A C N
DIADEM INFRINGES CHUM
S O O B R O A E O
FORWARDLOOKING GYPSUM
S N E E T Y E T S

## No. 18

S C K T O O B P
ALANINE PARES ARRAYS
L N N N R G LIT I R
AWARD AVOCADO LAGOON
M D L N D N A H T
LIGAMENT UNIVERSITIES
O R C S S C
CROSSBOW T MATRIARCHY
A A O ADIOS I V U N
LIMB U T V M O BILIP
N BELIEVE CHARRED C
ETNA D R O T I OUST
R T E P HELLO E W E
BOTHERSOME L RESONATE
V L S A H T
RECEPTIONIST BESMIRCH
R R A T E O A N H
ASSENT SPARROW FUDGE
I C TWO T A I A O E
MOUTHY STEEL NERVOUS
N S O D G I R E

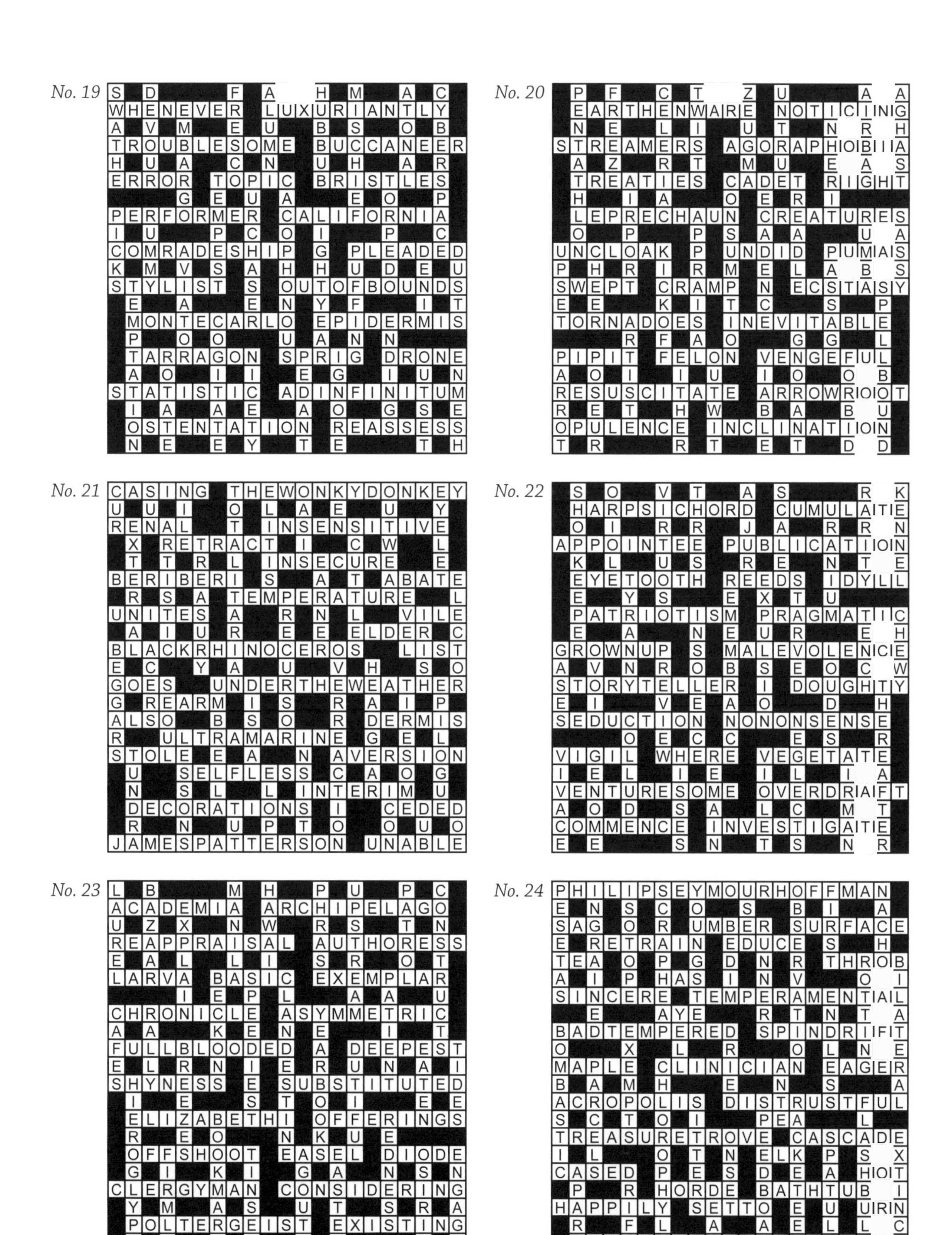
No. 19
No. 20
No. 21
No. 22
No. 23
No. 24

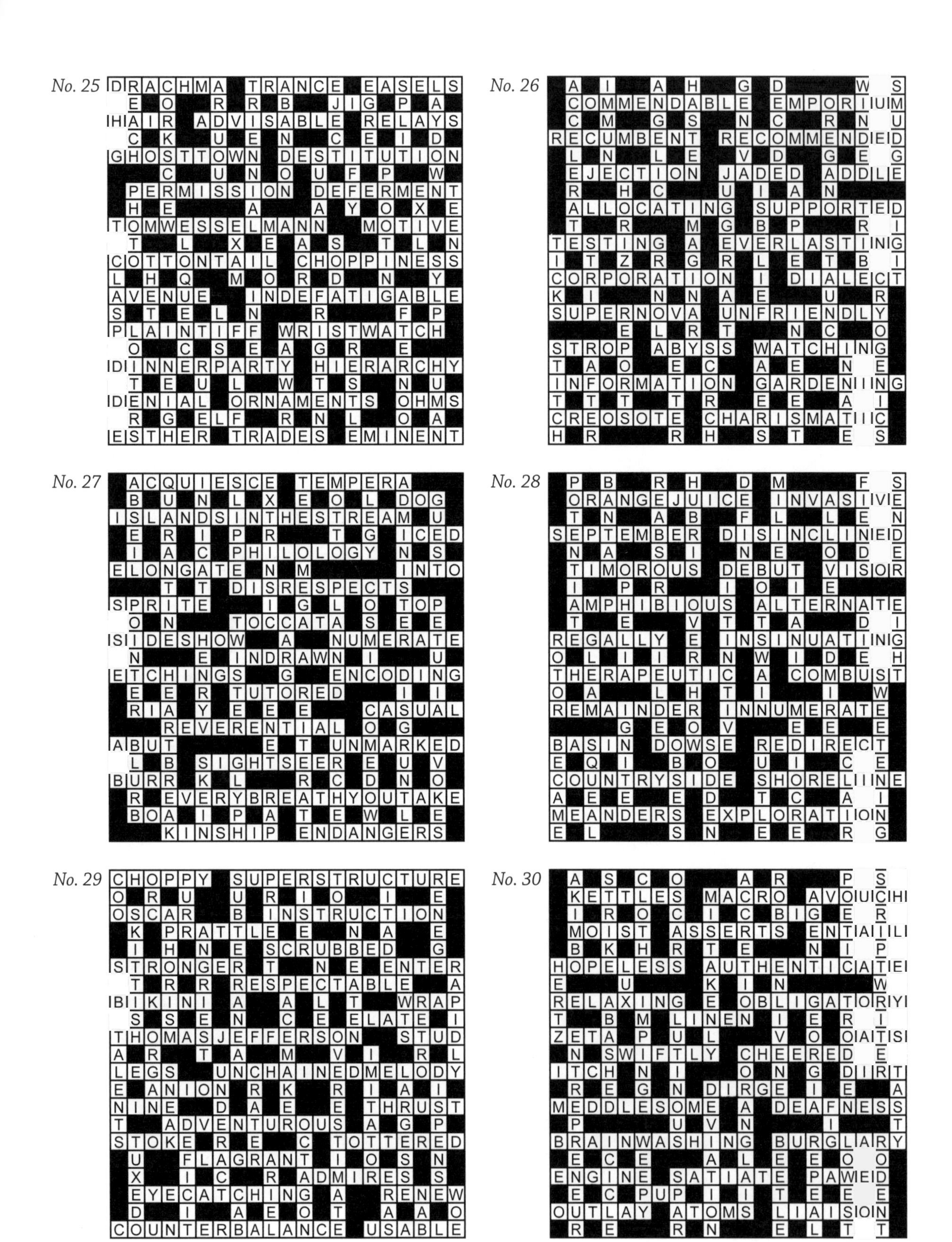

*No. 31*

A Q B S L B T E
SAUDIARABIA INFAMOUS
S O L L M O C R T
SEXTUPLET PICTURESQUE
M A E E N I R U E
BESOTTED SAUCE BREAM
L P I E N X I
INSPECTION CAPACITOR
E R N T O O H E
ESCHEWS S ENVIRONMENT
Q L S T T N E T E M R
UNOBSERVANT R STUPEFY
I S E N I E T L
PNEUMATIC ORDINARILY
E C E U U O B
DONOR HOSTS SEMINARY
E U I R H I E C N
BEASTIEBOYS TARPAULIN
T N E I M C A I G
OCCIDENT UPTOSCRATCH
R E S S M Y Y T

*No. 32*

ARUSHOFBLOODTOTHEHEAD
T N O L E R A A N X I
LOCATIONS ILLUSTRATES
A A T A I N L T A E D
SALIENT O OBESE PANDA
E L M IONIC S T S I
STEEPEN CONTRIBUTION
D E GAME D R V
REFER W B RETIREMENT
E O EVOLVE E O A A
ACRID P RUM M GRASP
M M I G ERASER N E
SLOPPINESS M D ASTIR
B I E BROW N I
BREASTSTROKE REDUCES
R D T I IRATE M I I
IBIZA BISON T CHOPPER
S E C R O G T K T A O
KINDHEARTED APATHETIC
E C I I T O I G E E C
THECOUNTOFMONTECRISTO

*No. 33*

BOW D K P S R B U U
R IKEBANA TEETER NOUN
A R N L G U C A R D
SHY THESOUNDOFSILENCE
H A I D R N A R
NIBBLED AIM DISSOLVES
E E O A E T A T
SCARVES MINOR ROMANIA
S N I C A T R T
BEDROOM ACCOMMODATE
F A E P B I E F S D
AGGLOMERATE TRAFFIC
M E M E S E R P
INDOORS STAID UPRAISE
L I C H I R B S
INDICATOR LOG EXPRESS
A D N E L M O I
ROBERTBADENPOWELL SUM
I A I D A B N I E I
TOLL LINEUP AUTOCUE S
Y S E D S L S Y PET

*No. 34*

AURICULAR LOVABLE
V E O I E I I R LAG
LEAVINGONAJETPLANE R
N E V N D E S CLUB
G R E EDINBURGH T E
DESSERTS N I OILY
I S SPECTACULAR
PEBBLE S E A I AMP
M L ASSURES Z T E
SIDESTEP N TRAVESTY
R H RECITAL R R
SANTIAGO T ENDORSED
T R N PAPYRUS E L
EWE K O O A DESIST
BESTSELLING O E
OPAL A N ISOLATES
R E TOPDRAWER R R M
ZINC A E A D B C P
E LARGETORTOISESHELL
DUE O V A E N L E O
FATTEST REGULARLY

*No. 35*

R W B S J C D A
EVENTUAL THOUGHTLESS
F A O I E M A A S
OBSERVATORY PATTERNED
R E N H E E R T S
MALTA VENOM DROUGHTS
D I E O O E M
PETROLEUM LASTMINUTE
E I W A L E E N
COMPETENTLY N CARROTS
K I L R O C E E I R I
SADDLES D OBSTRUCTION
U I E D C T O G
DISPLEASED EXISTENCE
I S X L N F E
TIMELESS ENTRY EPOCH
O U G U I E N B E
CROSSBEAM IMMEDIATELY
I T T M B K G Y D
UNEQUIVOCAL ETCETERA
M R C N E D D Y

*No. 36*

C I P B S N R W C
CHANEL ALPHANUMERIC
O S E S I R V T R
URGE ANTELOPES ERSATZ
E C I L E ERR O
MONTHS LOSER R I A O
G C L UNYIELDING
BREATHLESS R U S
A N O HUT HER L
POTPOURRI HAY ENAMEL
H H L U FAR M P T L
BYGONE NUT EXECUTIVE
L DUO SPA B O C
C O F DESALINATE
LINGUISTIC U I R
N Y N H OPALS CANYON
N TOE I C P E L
HAIRDO MONOTREME TOYS
M E N I I N L T S
CONSTELLATIONS KELVIN
N T D L N E S E S

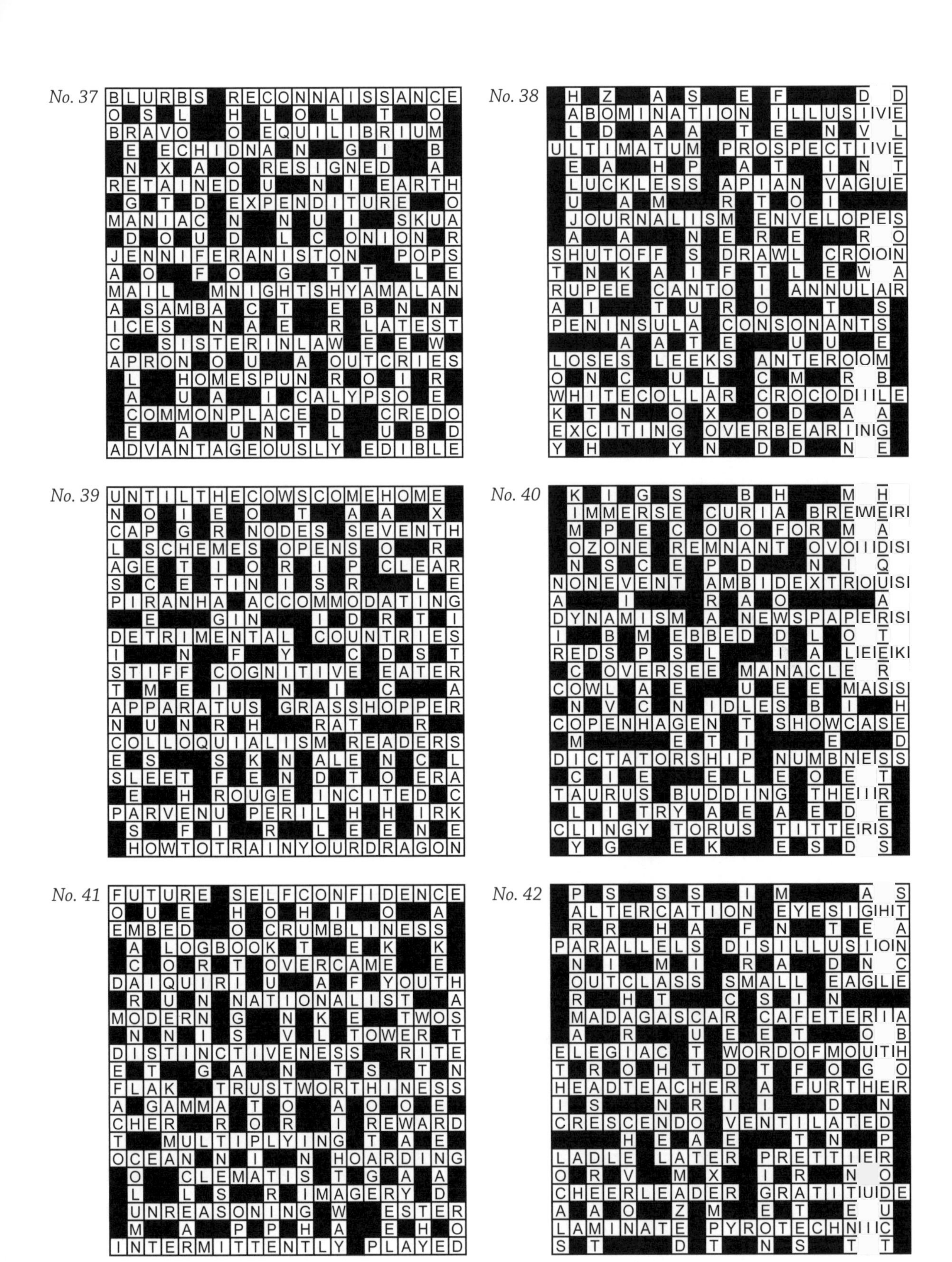
No. 37
No. 38
No. 39
No. 40
No. 41
No. 42

*No. 43*

THEPRINCEANDTHEPAUPER
Y Q E O R I R R V E E
PLUNDERER BUENOSAIRES
I I H M A B A D L E O
CALDERA N LUCRE ANNUL
A A R LATHE L N N V
LITERAL IRRESPECTIVE
E I YARD A H A
HERON C E BESTSELLER
A A GENERA R E E E
SALES E WOO N PACKS
T K V A ORATOR O E
ESPECIALLY K R OUGHT
L O D LOKI B N
TRANSPARENCY CALLOUS
H Y T L ANKLE E S P
ULTRA PLUMB I COMICAL
N H R L S I R R A E U
DEIFICATION SWEETENER
E N C Z O E C A I T G
RAGEAGAINSTTHEMACHINE

*No. 44*

A V W T U U R E E
AFRICA SUPERINTENDENT
F C R U B I C I G
WEPT MANNEQUIN INTERN
C I A A R T I P A
ATOMIC MUTED E E C V
I H I UNRESERVED
COMPRESSED E A D
N A E ARC SPY F
ALGORITHM HIT INTACT
T E I O SKI E E S O
REGAIN GOO MIDDLEMAN
N GEE NEE D A T
R T T STATIONARY
THOROUGHLY T N A
E Y P E UNCUT GUARDS
T SIR A A A L I
BONSAI NONENTITY INCH
R I L E V N E C T
WILDGOOSECHASE ABIDED
C E N S S D R A D

*No. 45*

CLAMPS TELECONFERENCE
O T E R E O E E O
BLESS A TYPEWRITERS
E COCONUT E E R M
C A L S UNDERLIE O
STANDOFF C U O ANGST
U S I ELECTRICITY U
BRAINS R O E A MARS
E O T A A K TRIPS S
BRANDENBURGGATE HILL
O B R L U R S D E
GOOF LEVELHEADEDNESS
G VIOLA I A N P O U
LIEN K C T S ABOARD
E ABSENTEEISM R N R
SADLY S O G INACTION
C ACIDRAIN S T I U
A N D R INSTEAD N
CANDLELIGHT I VENDS
I B E U E O O I H
CARLYRAEJEPSEN TWELVE

*No. 46*

O K D F R F W D
FANCIER BREVE SCORES
F I A O A S RAY M V
INGOT LECTERN RIBBED
S H O I K N I A L
RHYTHMIC SATISFACTION
A U T F A P
THOUGHTS R ULTIMATUMS
E N A ATOLL U E O E
SITE I N K R M ACNE
N ABRIDGE OMNIBUS T
STAR C P C I E TOSS
E T U A PECAN R E C
ARCHETYPAL I ENSHRINE
M E E D E N
BELLIGERENCE ABUNDANT
D O N T N D M E O
SIENNA AVERTED PATIO
A G WIG O A U I A S
GREETS USUAL CORNICE
Y D E S E E N S

*No. 47*

A M E I R P T R
BLIZZARD MANUFACTURE
A R A D P B S R S
CEREMONIOUS RETRIEVER
U O B E T I R E N
SPREE ASPEN CLARINET
Z M R O M N M
VENTILATE NEGLIGIBLE
O O Z V S A T N
DOMESTICATE L WEIGHTS
K A T N L N L I A E M
ADDLING E SCINTILLATE
I M N I V L R L
FUTURISTIC ANECDOTAL
F L D A N S E
ENTIRETY LOTUS SITES
R I N A R N C H E
REALISTIC EGALITARIAN
N I I H A O N N A
CONNOTATION AIRTIGHT
E G Y S S D S E

*No. 48*

P L D U D W J R
DONORS OWNER EPICURE
L C MUG S O P T N B
DEBATE SECLUDE HAIKU
P T L A N N I O F
DOMESTICATED DANDRUFF
S O H A I U
DISSIDENCE B SHIPPING
T P E D DROLL N L U
TIERED U U U D APSE
O A UNCLE TAG E T P
SNOW C T V G PREFIX
O L E OVERT A T A C
CRUSADER R EARTHQUAKE
K S Y N D A
SPARKLED TRANSCENDENT
L E U R H C L E D
USING ORIGINS UNLESS
N G G O N O POD U P
GENTEEL GAUZE ENDEAR
E S D S S D E N

*No. 49*

GAB P U W S O B G I
O LEARNER PAPAYA RAIN
L E R S I U E L A T
DEW COUNTERPRODUCTIVE
M E S H A S E M
ENVELOP EGG BUTTERCUP
D E E R L R A E
AEROBIC TWICE WAVERER
L B L T O E D A
OBELISK FLABBERGAST
S S A N Y U O O B E
PRESTIGIOUS RHOMBUS
R N U A G O E S
INROADS LAPEL INTENSE
N O I I E E C N
GATHERING RAW WAITERS
C O E N E O C I
LESPECTREDELAROSE FAT
E P T O W V G B O I
ACRE LEGUME EPITOME V
N D Y S R S E X SUE

*No. 50*

B L R U E W H U
EMOTION MEDIA SKIING
R U D M E U DEN C B
LIVED ARTICLE EXCEED
I R L S I A E U L
KNEEJERK CATASTROPHIC
I I U I U E
TROUBLES L OPPRESSIVE
E N A THORN E X I A
SILK M E U R P LOBS
N EMBLEMS MOSELLE L
ATOM A P A E O NEED
R P D N PINED D C U
CONTRAVENE A EXEGESIS
D S R G E T
BUSINESSLIKE SYMMETRY
C R R M M T O S U
STROBE THEREBY RACES
O N COY T N L B R H
ORIENT PLEAT EPISODE
Y D E R S D W D

*No. 51*

J A I C G D T A
UNTHINKABLE OUTSTRIP
G T V U M G O U P
EGREGIOUS BIBLIOPHILE
E N I E N E R S N
REDFACED SINGS AIMED
N L E T O O N
AMBASSADOR CORMORANT
U T A O T T L O
STRATUM U NOURISHMENT
E E E A G G R E U R E
PARTNERSHIP N SANCTUM
A U T T O A D N
LANDSLIDE ILLSTARRED
C N R N R E R
AUDIO INSET ANECDOTE
S E U I N D A U S
SOVEREIGNTY DESPOTISM
I O E G I L U F I
SQUIRREL CELEBRATION
I T E E D E T G

*No. 52*

MOB P P B W D A C R
E UNAWARE OSIERS HAVE
L O E R D O S S A S
BAY LOOKBEFOREYOULEAP
O L C U U R E L
UNLEASH GYM PROTOTYPE
R I I O T M A N
NAMIBIA ORCAS DECAPOD
E P L L W H N E
OPINION ATTESTATION
A P T S E U E S S T
BRONZEMEDAL SALUTES
B X O K F E U T
REJECTS CAGES EARLIER
E O R L I M N A
VEGETABLE COD PLUNGED
I X N A A L P E
ATTHEELEVENTHHOUR DIM
T A O I O L Y E O A
EVIL URANUS IRELAND R
D E S G Y A D R OAK

*No. 53*

F Z I M F O P C
IDEALISM AUDIOVISUAL
N P I P S S E T O
INHABITANTS CORROSIVE
S Y E L I A T C E
HIRER PARCH LAUNCHER
I E E E R O L
SARCASTIC ATTENDANCE
T I R O V O R A
ESSENTIALLY L CASTOFF
E K A F L H E A E B I
RESPRAY E ACRIMONIOUS
L R C N A E E T
ASSOCIATED NARCISSUS
S W M E C A L
TRESPASS DREGS LACED
I X G E I A I A R
ACCORDION ADOLESCENCE
I D N I G L I A N
TOURDEFORCE ESOTERIC
Y S D R D Y D H

*No. 54*

P M A C S B D P
FLOORS STREW TREMOLO
A S WOK U H A A L N
DYNAMO SUCKING RELIC
W I O I T E E A H
DISCONSOLATE DARKROOM
T F L D I U
THOUGHTFUL W SOFTBALL
F T U S YEAST R L C
LINEAR P R A A EACH
R N DARED FUR N O
NETS L I I B TEDIUM
O I E NOVEL O I E R
BULLFROG I INACCURATE
L E N S R M
EXPEDITE ANTEDILUVIAN
E A D N T E A E R
RURAL FEIGNED WARMTH
X T I O O E AWN N I
ETHANOL NORMS SCALAR
S S G D S H L L

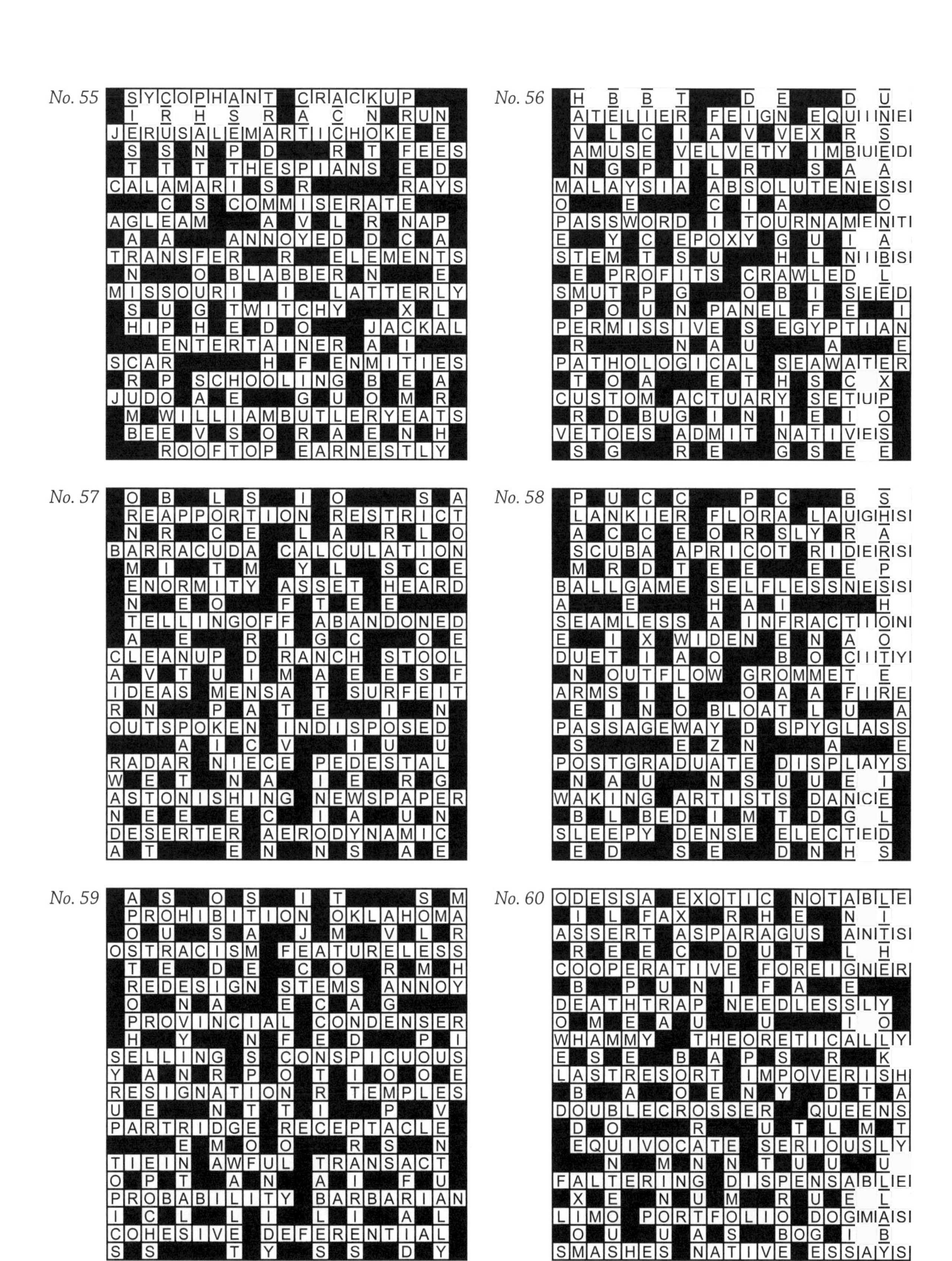

*No. 61*

D T D L R S C T
SEARCH ALOHA OUTDOES
T I IVY N N N E L E
DEEPEN SIGHTED PILOT
R L T I A O P A S
IMPERSONATOR SHERRIES
I E U C O I
UNDERSTOOD T ARRESTED
A N A L EMITS A I L
ABLOOM O C S V TOME
L U URGES ALIBI D I
BEAN R I P G OBOIST
E C A SWARM N L W A
SOLECISM C AFICIONADO
E U E T N V
TRIPPING SLEDGEHAMMER
A R N R H R E U N
STOOD EDIFICE ASTUTE
C O U A P A N I T I U
AFFECTS SOLID HUNGRY
L S E E S S Y E

*No. 62*

A B A P A R I B
INGOTS LYRIC DREAMIER
T B PIT A O V C P O
BAMBOO OCCLUDE AGAIN
G I R T N R L I C
COUNTERPOINT BALLROOM
N L C R E O
PINACOLADA Y MASTERED
S W B T LEMMA C R E
STEAKS F A D O ORBS
I R COOED NOD R S I
ACID U R I E POISON
N E R MERGE N I O G
GOODNESS E SHIPOWNERS
R A C P N A
YOUNGEST TRIGGERHAPPY
D O S I I O O T H
DROOP GROANED OUTBID
E D R E N A ELM A C
SOLDIER SAGES SOCIAL
T E T S E K K L

*No. 63*

S T A U S S V S
APHRODISIAC EMISSARY
N W J H A E H R D
ADVANTAGE PREMONITION
W R C R A L A E E
INTEGERS OBEYS TODAY
C C N B R Y S
HAILSTORMS RESOURCES
E I E T O T U I
USURPED M RINSE HABIT
T N S E I U E M I A
TEASE PANIC O SIDECAR
E R R I T U E B
REMEMBERS INSANDOUTS
E S C V E U O
RIVEN SIEGE FRUITFUL
E O A M I L R O U
SKYSCRAPERS EXONERATE
O A E A D D T A I
REGISTER LAUGHINGGAS
T E T E E C E M

*No. 64*

A S E C S C R B
POCKETMONEY ALLELUIA
O R H U M V P D R
ACOUSTICS OBSESSIVELY
A F O I O I S S O
LIFESPAN CLANG TITAN
Y N I O R R L
PLAGIARISM GEOMETRIC
S A N F E U A H
DEMIGOD C OMNIPOTENCE
I U E E R R T E E G S
VIRIDESCENT I DIMNESS
E A P A A N P E
DELIRIOUS BLANKETING
O I E L I E M
TYING LEDGE BACKDATE
Y S U R L E K R N
PROVISIONAL FABRICATE
I B S D N A A T I
SEASHORE DUPLICATION
T R D S L K C G

*No. 65*

CROCHET MAGNUM SLOUCH
O O I Y E ARE R L
OMEN AMUSINGLY CRIMEA
E C P T U O T B A
COLONNADE IMPRESSIONS
R N R N L L O S
INDECISIVE UNABASHED
M A E G N P A E
TASTELESSNESS HOBNOB
G S P A M C P O U
CONSTRAINT ENLIVENING
O I A N A A E R O
BONOBO GLORIFICATION
R T L S E R R K
ATHEISTIC WORLDCLASS
S S I K E E C
FURTHERMORE GRAVITATE
N A M O K U D A R
CALLUP GONDOLIER BAIT
M O TAU A A N L T
KIDNEY LAWYER SLEEPER

*No. 66*

T S A T C M F C
ROCKANDROLL APOSTATE
A H G A I N H C L
INTERESTS IMAGINATIVE
S M T H A E R A R
INAHURRY EXERT INLAY
S U O X D R N
TANTAMOUNT INAUGURAL
O C N R T D E A
CRASHED L ALONE BLUNT
U V E U I P R R A S C
TEAMS LIMBO I SCREECH
U I L I L A B R
POLLUTANT ALLEGRETTO
M R E T Y L S
PLUMP DODGE BURGLARS
A N T O E R A P R
SELFEVIDENT AUTOMATION
T I E L T N I T A
REKINDLE LOUDMOUTHED
Y E S Y S N Y S

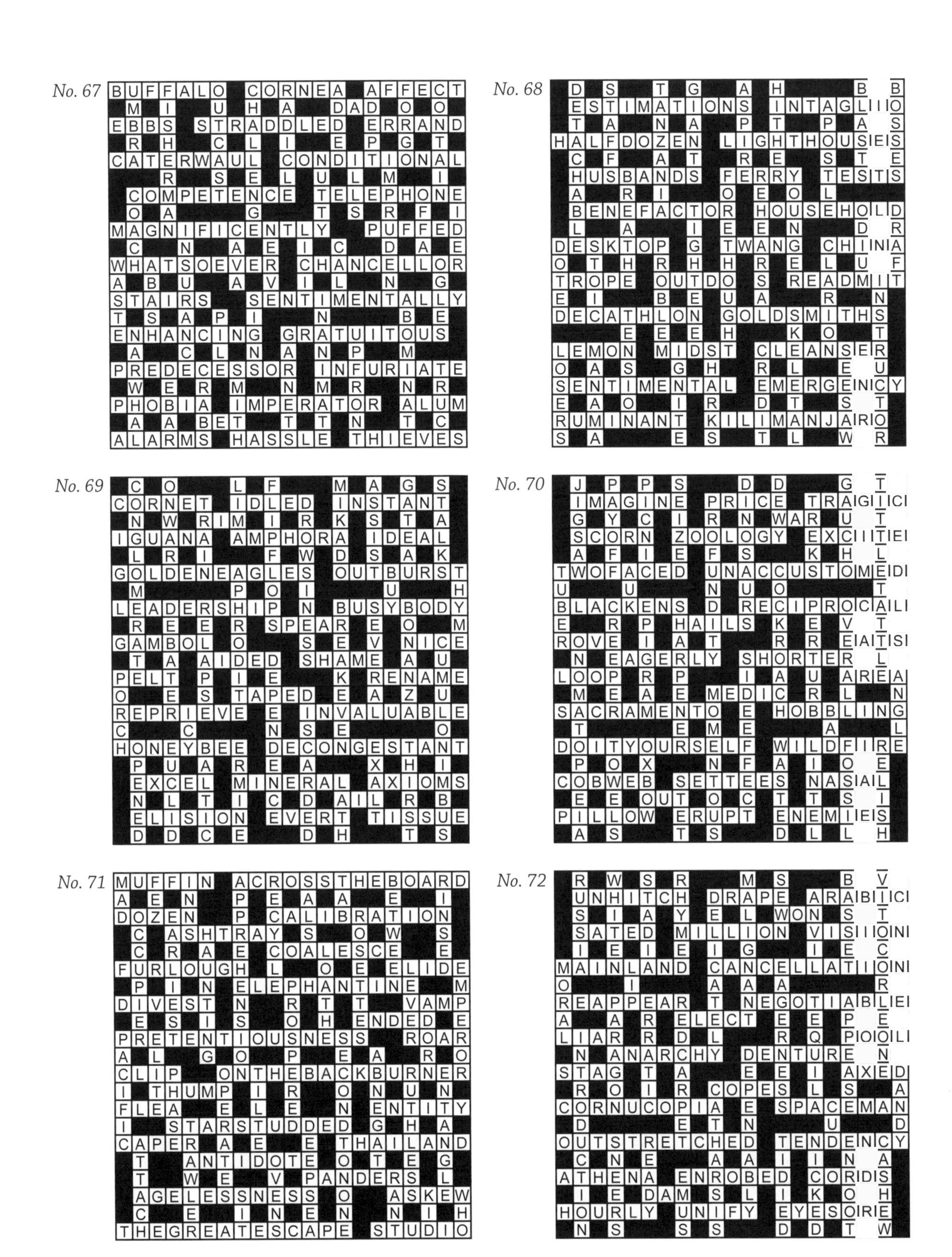
No. 67
No. 68
No. 69
No. 70
No. 71
No. 72

## No. 73

C V A I G E U G
BLOUSE RANTS AMMONIA
O L BIT S A L I T Z
STUCCO STOICAL NAIVE
H A N M R O E E B
PENNSYLVANIA NAMEDROP
S A I M E A
CHINCHILLA E CHILDREN
O I E U CONGA L O G
FRUGAL E T R L GEMS
S E POLES SIEVE F Y
BEAR I E C T GUILTY
R I N SCRUB A A S H
ENLARGES A LIKELIHOOD
W U T I E L
SLUGGISH CONGREGATION
O O N U H D L R G
CIVIC SNIFFED ITALIC
U E H T N O ODD I C
SURREAL GULLS EXTRAS
T N S E D E S L

## No. 74

COMMANDED WARSHIP
L I M I E A E O SKY
PERCYBYSSHESHELLEY E
R R I T Y K D CRAG
I O T ADDRESSES H R
SCISSION R P OWNS
C O TRADITIONAL
SHOOIN T C N U OWE
O P TRESSED R G P
FLUENTLY T ESSAYIST
L E PARADOX E I
KALAHARI I ENSEMBLE
N N S STARRED A O
DIN E T V A HONING
ILLUSIONIST A U
WISH I L ABRASIVE
N I GRANDPRIX A C E
IDOL E R O I N R I
I ALEVELPLAYINGFIELD
APT S N O D N U P E
ELEGANT SUGGESTED

## No. 75

P S S S D W L S
STENCIL FLESH SCATHE
Y A R I L L YAWN A
COMMA CREDITS INCURS
H A P E U G R E P
SEINFELD REHABILITATE
C R D T O O
ANALYTIC E EXORBITANT
R E H RULED T U E G
PICA I I I S R ROUT
M RECITES CATERER E
PAN K I A R I AIDE
R E L Q VOLGA T C S
OWDOYOUDO C PROJECTS
V E L U A A
METAPHYSICAL DROWSILY
M D E A A I F M I
ERAIL SENATES FLING
N P MAW O E P S L H
TATUS AMEND EVEREST
S S M S L T S S

## No. 76

P I S H A D L R
ATMOSPHERIC OFFSHORE
T P L C U L H N A
CROISSANT SMALLMINDED
I S T I E O M O E
ATHLETIC INEPT MINER
R A E M Q H E
CONCERTINA UNEARTHED
H O N G I O E O
SYNONYM H IMPERSONATE
C O I U A N M E D V R
ABRACADABRA E MADNESS
N S D I T N M P
SPEARMINT INTERWEAVE
E E E O O N C
SEEDS RADON GAUNTLET
C N C I P L L A A
HOSPITALITY AWESTRUCK
E U N I I N T V L
MARKDOWN CONCATENATE
E E G S E E E S

## No. 77

MAT P A A D N H B S
E WHISPER ALUMNA OATH
R I N P I F M N L O
COG CHRISTTHEREDEEMER
U E E E R M R T
REBIRTH SAT ANAEROBIC
I O E U L D A H
ARTISAN LINKS ROTUNDA
L A E S I I W N
NAGGING COMMINGLING
V I U V H A N O N E
INCREMENTAL DIVERGE
N O A L E S P B
DEFRAUD SOPPY REENTRY
I I T O A T L S
CATECHISM ZOO ENCRYPT
A X O E P B U A
THEHORSEWHISPERER BUN
I O G H B O A T A D
OVER ALKALI SETTLER E
N T N T S E E Y BAR

## No. 78

P P S E S C G T
ECLECTIC DRAWTHELINE
N A H A I E U M R
CONSIDERATE RETAILERS
I E A C O V Z E A
LATIN ZEBRA EMPHATIC
T I E R A I O
COMMINGLE INCOHERENT
I E Z K S L S T
TRANSPARENT I ETHICAL
E T P G E O E M I R I
SLYNESS P CONTEMPLATE
I C E R T R N N
KOOKABURRA EXACTNESS
E L L C L L A
MOLECULE YIELD NESTS
I Y S N M O K K I
ENERGETIC APPLICATION
D I E A U L R I G
ENCOURAGING EVIDENCE
D S Y E N D G D

## *No. 79*

PRIMING FACING SISTER
A A I L O LOT T L
EDEN ANNAPURNA ADORES
I I S T R Z S R M
CONFIDENT ANTECHAMBER
E N E G O U M N
RESURGENCE NORMALITY
O T E I D Z M A
HYPOCHONDRIAC REPAIR
A R O O R G M G D
CLAVICHORD SHARPENERS
U N T N E O T N O
BUDGIE COUNTERATTACK
E E C R L A H K
DESTITUTE DISPOSSESS
Y S I A I T B S
DENOMINATOR ENJOYABLE
B U S M T L E U A
DAMSEL INCIDENCE RIGS
L T EAT E S T U E
CLOSET YEARNS SENSORY

## *No. 80*

E S E O F U I E C
EXITED BROBDINGNAGIAN
C A G S R D S G S
CHUB EMERGENCE INSTEP
A L R E O RID M
UNBEND VERSE S E E E
G E E SATISFYING
TERRAFIRMA A E T
A E E BOY FIN O
BINOCULAR OFF OSPREY
L D T I ADD E F E L
MERINO FAD ENDURANCE
T RYE ELL I E C
A I S SIMILARITY
ABSOLUTELY U L R
H N N N ACTED SUBMIT
O TOT K E D A F
CRAFTY ESSENTIAL KEYS
R A I N N E A E I
JEANINECUMMINS PARENT
D S G E S T S Y G

## *No. 81*

S J S P T S S L
CHOREOGRAPH TENTACLE
R Y U E O Y E E N
AUTOPILOT TRAMPOLINES
P U M T A I A E E
UNSTEADY EXPEL VESTS
L R T M R A I
OBLITERATE EQUIVOCAL
U M R R P N R I
ASSUMED C GRANDCANYON
R I E E H E R E N P E
MALEDICTION I ROTATED
E O O T C N H N
DISCOURSE INGREDIENT
T U C E T L E
COMET MYTHS UPHOLDER
O O O O A P E R T
WELLMEANING PARABOLAS
B T A D G I E P I
ONEONONE ABSTRACTION
Y N R R Y L N S

## *No. 82*

C M A I R N B S
PANAMA LINGO ACETONE
B K PIG D V N C O N
GIVEUP AGELESS TABOO
N D L L R O A O R
AERODYNAMICS MARJORAM
T N B H O A
IMMATERIAL A GESTURES
A T C M YODEL I P K
SKETCH A O A L SEAS
E E OATHS WED I W P
DRAM I I O I CREEPS
E P N OILED A O P R
PENTAGON I EXTINCTION
T N D S O A
HUMIDITY IMPERTINENCE
N N N U F A R X H
SIGHS CUISINE OCULAR
E E E C E R MAN D B
AUSTRIA DREAM SPELLS
T T T S D Y S E

## *No. 83*

V I A U P S E R B A P
I MONGREL VIENNA NERO
E I R E A E S C N R
WAD EMMELINEPANKHURST
P S E O O G A R
OMITTED MAY NEURALGIA
I N I E S O E I
NEGLECT BLAZE QUARTET
T R E A U R N I
AERATED SECONDGUESS
E I I E G O O L N T
DINNERDRESS CONTORT
U E A K A O R B
COEXIST DITTY LUMBAGO
A T O E Y C N D
TRANSLATE REV OUTSTAY
I U U P I H I G
OPERATIONOVERLORD GNU
N S I E I A L I A A
ACHE ORISON GLIDERS R
L D N S E O C S HID

## *No. 84*

E L I S B S C V
CRIMINOLOGY TOILSOME
O Q T A L O A W N
INCUMBENT KILLERWHALE
O O G E N E S R E
MURMURED FERNS UNDER
I I A O E P I
CORNFLOWER SHORTENED
A U I E T N U O
FLATTER T FORTS FERAL
E N E E H A A O I S L
TOGAS AUDIT I REGRESS
C E P R H N H E
HARMONICA ESTIMATION
U N W R O E T
PLAIT GENES LITERATI
U I D N I O H N M
MIRRORIMAGE SUBSISTED
I I N I H I A W N
CANOEIST TRANSLUCENT
E G Y H G L R S

*No. 85*

T S T O A S A B
AQUILINE CONDITIONER
S P A R C S A Y O
TREACHEROUS OARSWOMAN
E R K O R R D N D
DUBAI CRASH BOULDERS
N H S I S E H
RELIGIONS DEACTIVATE
U I I A E C E E
CONJUNCTIVA C MALLETS
K E G E L N E O O N T
STROLLS A DISCREPANCY
A I N S S O U L
BLUEBOTTLE INCLUSIVE
E S I E O C N
REPTILES KENDO COCOA
N O I C V I H H N
CAPTAINCY CASTIGATION
C A E T D H I E U
LITHOSPHERE EVENTFUL
E O S E S R S S

*No. 86*

*No. 87*

ABSORB UNCLOG OUTSIDE
A S ION I L P I I
ENSIGN INEBRIATE GIVE
S E G T E S I H E
THERMOMETER SECRETARY
E A E U A A A L
MEDICINAL LONELINESS
A E A D I D S E
NOBODY PREPOSSESSING
N T A L O O O P S
ASSUMPTION SUBTRACTED
T I N D E S G H W
MARGARETCOURT THRICE
M U O A T E E L
PRIMADONNA BEAUTIFUL
D E V S L X T N
PINEAPPLE PRECIPITOUS
N L L R H L Y O S
SARI CONTRALTO LAWFUL
N N Y E L TOO N A
VENEERS DETACH NESTLE

*No. 88*

BUS L D S E E A R O
L CHALICE CAVIAR AJAR
O A M L R H A C B C
WIN BEATAROUNDTHEBUSH
T D P P E B I E
ORIGAMI HEM SEMIOTICS
R G D A C S L T
CANASTA ALGAE CHECKER
H O T T G I O A
ROOMIER CHIROPODIST
S E M O E S S G D E
INDEPENDENT SETFREE
G Q O U E E A A
NONPLUS ATONE NESTLES
I O E U L T L C
FURNISHED SEC ANODYNE
I O T I H T U N
CONVERSATIONALIST HAD
A E I I D N O P E I
NULL ABROAD COUTURE N
T S N N S E S T DIG

*No. 89*

A O R D M A F A
KNIVES AVERS EMPTIES
N E TUG L A S I G P
SOIREE SHIELDS EXUDE
U D W V U U C R C
INCONSEQUENT PREVENTS
C U R A E T
CENTIGRADE T PITTANCE
M R A R DRIVE R T E
REVEAL T O P I LAUD
N M INERT NIP U A N
STUB L R E E MENTAL
A L E LURKS R P T T
CEREMONY M TOOTHPASTE
K U I A N A
SOLIDITY NARCISSISTIC
B M O O A G W N N
TEPID UMBRAGE AVATAR
U O I T L Z LAY Z B
SCRUNCH EVENS SIZZLE
E T E S R E Y E

*No. 90*

I B I C E B D S I
SNAILS ALCATRAZ ISLAND
C A L R H T S I S
FOGS ECOLOGIST OUTLAW
N E U E T LOW N
ASIDES SEDGE E N D I
O T E MAGISTRATE
BLOWBYBLOW R A Y
A I L ROB OWL M
BELLICOSE YOU UGANDA
L L S C AMP N N T E
DESPOT CUT ADDICTION
O SEA HAS H S U
S W S SERPENTINE
SCREECHING U O C
U R O O URBAN NORDIC
L DON L Y N A A
SPIRAL APPREHEND FITS
T E I L B R E F I
SOMEONELIKEYOU FOLLOW
R D G Y E P Y E N

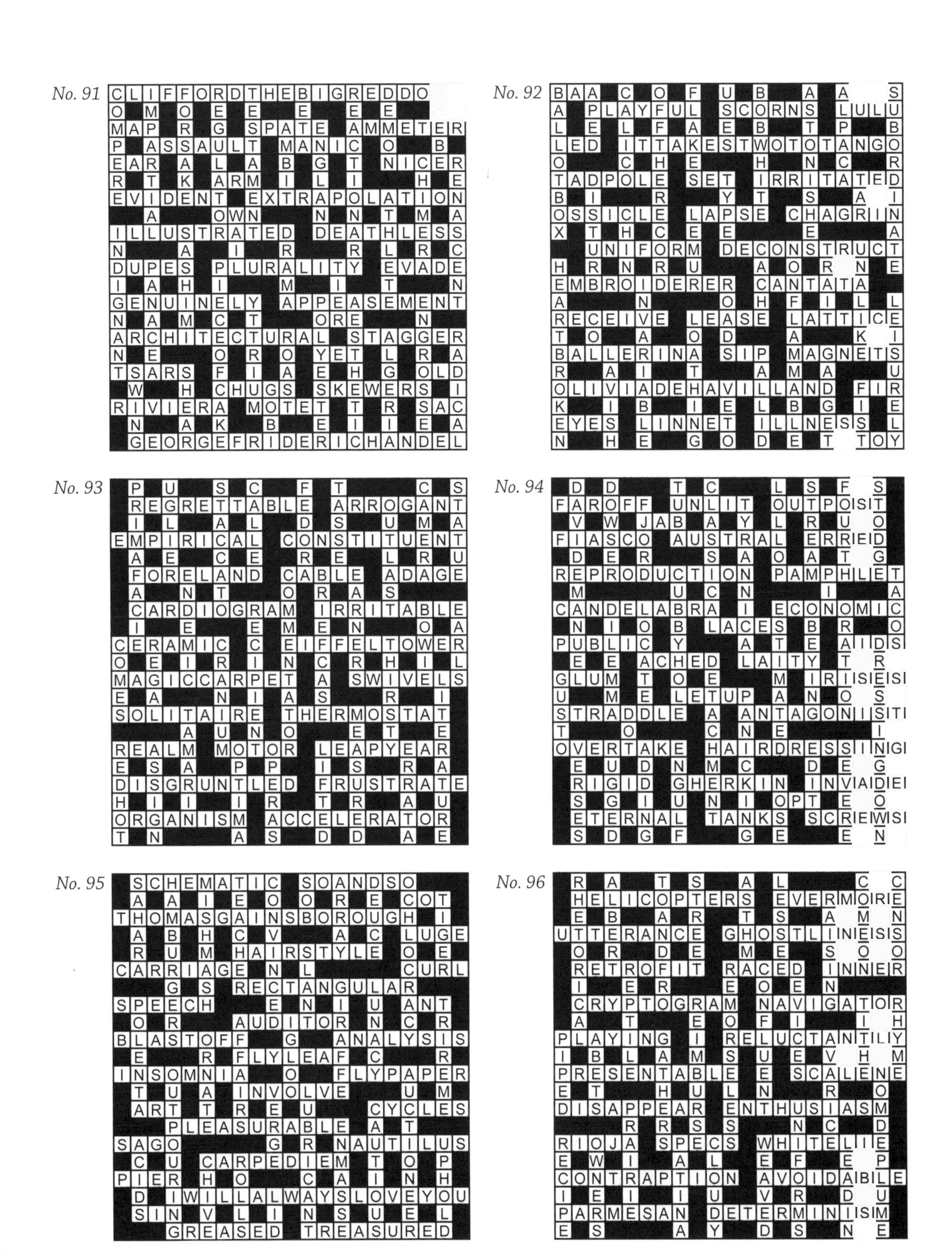

*No. 97*

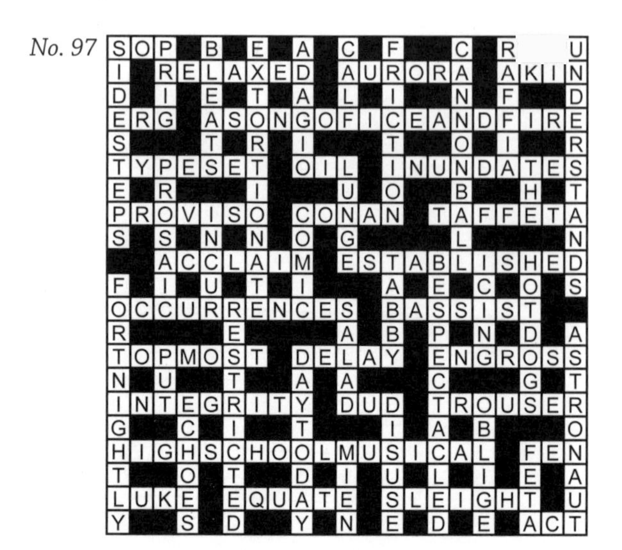

*No. 98*

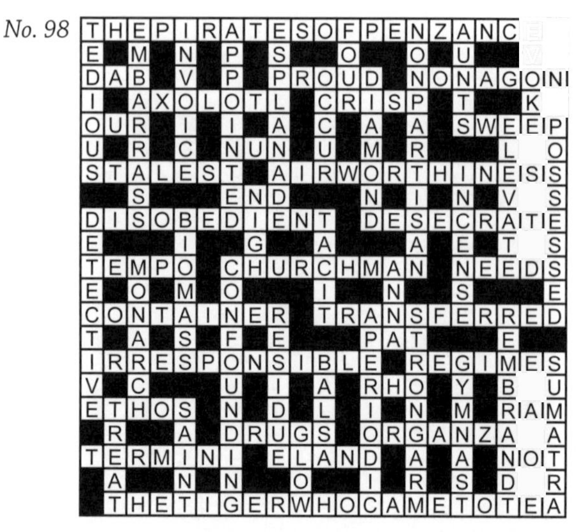

*No. 99*

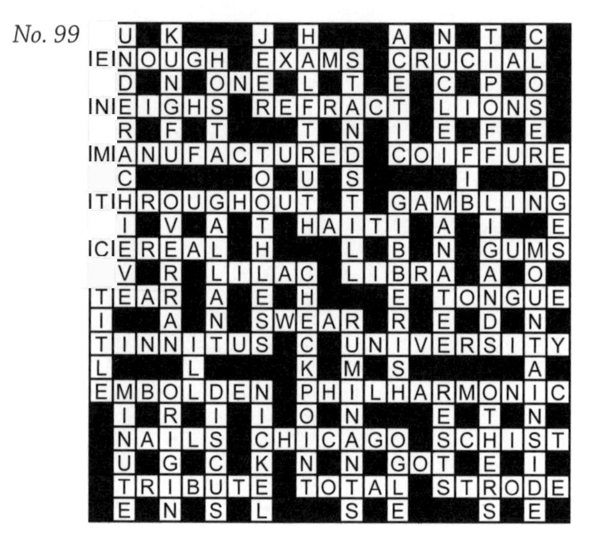

*No. 100*

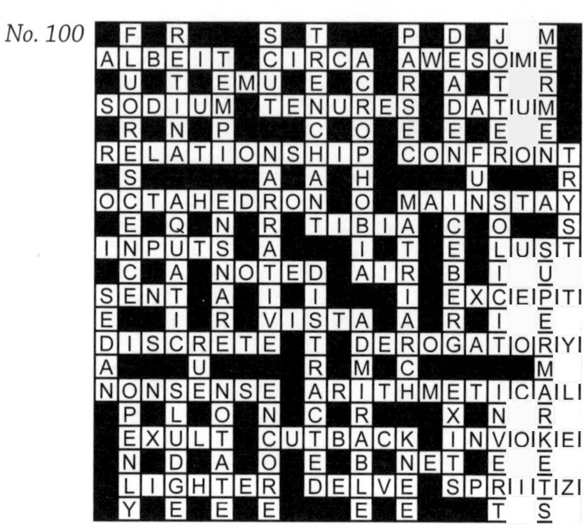